From Texians to Texans
The Birth of Texas

James R. Bower

Copyright © 2025 James R. Bower

All rights reserved. No part of this book may be reproduced or transmitted in any form or by any means, electronic or mechanical, including photocopying, recording or by any information storage and retrieval system without permission in writing from the publisher.

Average Dog Publishing–Deer Park, TX
Paperback ISBN: 979-8-9921872-0-5
eBook ISBN: 979-8-9921872-1-2
Library of Congress Control Number: 2024927491
Title: *From Texians to Texans: The Birth of Texas*
Author: James R. Bower
Digital distribution | 2025
Paperback | 2025

Published in the United States by New Book Authors Publishing

Table of Contents

Chapter 1: Texas Revolution 1
Chapter 2: The Alamo Mission................................. 9
Chapter 3: The Battle of the Alamo........................ 14
Chapter 4: Excerpts and List of Defenders............. 32
Chapter 5: Battle of San Jacinto 47
Chapter 6: William B. Travis.................................. 52
Chapter 7: James Bowie 58
Chapter 8: Davy Crockett 70
Chapter 9: Sam Houston 82
Chapter 10: Santa Anna 98
Chapter 11: Mexican-American War.................... 117
Credits for Reference 119
About the Author 120

Chapter One
Texas Revolution

Having won its independence from Spain in 1821, the underdeveloped Republic of Mexico sought to gain control of its northern reaches which, under the Spanish, had functioned as an extensive and largely empty wall against advancement by competing French and British Empires to the north. That northern region, which became the state of Coahuila and Texas under fire from the federal system, created by the Mexican Constitution of 1824, was scarcely populated by Mexicans and dominated by Native American people, the Apache and the Comanche. Because a lot of Mexican people were reluctant to move there, the Mexican Government offered Americans and other foreigners to settle there exempting them from certain tariffs and taxes for seven years under the Imperial Colonization Law of January 1823. Mexico banned slavery in 1829, but allowed American immigrant slaveholders to continue using the labor of enslaved people.

Among those who made the most of the opportunity to settle in Texas were Americans Green DeWitt and Moses Austin. They were given the title Empresario by being granted large tracts of land on which to establish colonies of hundreds of families. Moses Austin died before he could begin establishing the colonies but his son, Stephen Austin, led a militia, in 1826, and aided the Mexican military in an early attempt at securing independence from Mexico by settlers in the area near Nacogdoches that had resulted from a conflict between old settlers and those who came as part of the grant to Hayden Edwards.

"COME TAKE IT"

Green DeWitt feared for the safety of the colony. The Impresario of the DeWitt Colony had led 400 Americans to settle in the Mexican Territory of Texas near the Junction of the San Marcos and Guadalupe Rivers, in 1825, but since then, the capital of his colony, Gonzales, had been struck repeatedly by Native American raids and attacks.

In 1831, the Mexican government had provided Gonzales a small, 6 pound cannon that DeWitt had requested to defend the outpost. By September 1835, DeWitt had died and the Mexican Government found itself under General Antonio Lopez de Santa Anna, who had become the biggest security threat to the Texans (known as the Texians) in Gonzales.

Santa Ann soon transformed himself into a dictator, ultimately replacing the 1824 Constitution with a new document, The Seven Laws in 1836, that formally put power in the hands of those holding titles with qualifications established for holding office and voting, and restored the states military districts. Santa Anna showed no qualms about suppressing opinions as he did in the spring of 1835 in Zacatecas, in Mexico, where he overwhelmed the local militia and caused damage in the area for some 48 hours. September, of that year, he claimed central control over Texas because he believed that the United States was going to acquire it by dispatching General Martin Perfecto de Cos to San Antonio with 300 to 500 troops.

With the relations between the Mexican Government and the American settlers deteriorating, Santa Anna gave orders to disarm the Texans, including repossessing the modest cannon provided to Gonzales four years earlier. The majority of those in Gonzales agreed to refuse the Mexican Government's order to immediately return the cannon.

At the end of September, the Mexican soldiers moved on Gonzales to retake the cannon that earlier they had given to the town for defense against attack by the Native Americans. The Mexican soldiers were halted at the Guadalupe River, near Gonzales, by eighteen militiamen.

A Mexican messenger swam across the river to get the reply from Gonzales Town Official, Joseph Clements, to another demand to turn over the cannon. Clements wrote, "I cannot now and will not deliver to you the cannon."

After the Texan forces gathered to outnumber the Mexicans, then challenged them to "Come Take It" [the cannon]. On October 2, they attacked and forced the Mexicans to retreat to San Antonio; this act was the Texas Revolutions first win, which came to be known as the Battle of Gonzales. By mid-October, Austin commanded a growing army and began the siege of San Antonio, on October 28, after fending off a Mexican attack and then successfully counterattacking in the Battle of Concepcion and winning the "Grass Fight" (a battle over a mule train carrying grass for the Mexican horses west of San Antonio).

Prelude to Battle

Colonel James C. Neill, who was the acting commander of the Alamo, wrote a letter to the Provisional Government stressing that they would be unable to withstand a siege lasting longer than four days. On January 14, Neill approached Sam Houston for assistance in gathering supplies, ammunition and clothing. Houston couldn't spare any number of men to mount a successful defense. Houston instead had Colonel James Bowie, with 30 men, destroy the Alamo and remove the artillery. Bowie was unable to remove the artillery due to the lack of animals at the Alamo garrison.

Neill persuaded Bowie that the Alamo held strategic importance. Bowie wrote a letter to Governor Henry Smith stating that the salvation of Texas depended on keeping Bexar out of the hands of the Mexican Army. The Alamo serves as the Frontier Military Post and if it were to fall into the possession of Santa Anna, there would be no way to stop him in his march towards Sabine.

Bowie's letter to Smith ended by saying, "Colonel Neill and I have come to the resolution that we will rather die in these ditches than give it up to the enemy." Bowie also wrote a letter to the Provisional Government requesting for rifles, men, money and cannon powder.

Only a few reinforcements were authorized. Officer William B. Travis arrived with thirty men, on February 3. Five days later, the famous frontiersman and former U.S. Congressman David Crockett and a few volunteers arrived.

Colonel James C. Neill, the Commander of the Alamo, left the garrison, likely, to recruit men and to gather supplies. In his absence, he left newcomers William B. Travis and Officer James Bowie in charge, who commanded a volunteer company. The men, instead, elected Bowie, who had the reputation as a fierce fighter, as their commander. Bowie got very intoxicated by celebrating and raised havoc in Bexar. To lessen the ill feelings, Bowie agreed to share command with Travis.

As the Texians struggled trying to recruit men and find supplies, Santa Anna was continuing to gather men. By the end of 1835, Santa Anna's army numbered over 6,000 soldiers.

Instead of Santa Anna advancing along the coastline where he could have reinforcements and supplies easily delivered by sea, he ordered his army to Bexar, which is the center of Texas. In late December, the army began its march north and the officers trained their men along the way. A lot of the new recruits didn't know how to aim their muskets and didn't want to fire from their shoulders because of the recoil. The record cold and snow, rationing of food, sickness and Comanche raids took a heavy toll on the Mexican soldiers.

On February 21, Santa Anna's army reached the Medina River, 25 miles from Bexar. Unaware of the Mexican Army's location, most of the Alamo's garrison had joined a fiesta going on in Bexar. Santa Anna, learning of the celebration, gave orders to seize the unprotected Alamo, but sudden rains stopped the raid.

A good friend of William B. Travis, a local resident, Ambrosia Rodriguez, warned him that a relative claimed that Santa Anna was on the march towards Bexar. Two days later, a scout of Juan Seguin, Blas Maria Herrera said the Mexican Army had crossed the Rio Grande. Travis seemed to ignore all the rumors of Santa Anna's arrival.

THE ALAMO

The Alamo
Location in Texas

Location: 300 Alamo Plaza
San Antonio, Texas, U.S.

Coordinates: 29°25'33"N 98°29'10"W

Name as founded: Mision San Antonio de Valero

English translation: Saint Anthony of Valero Mission

Patron: Anthony of Padua

Founding priest(s): Buenaventura y Oliver

Area: 5 acres (2.0 ha)

Built: 1718

Natives tribe(s): Coahuiltecans

Governing body: Texas General Land Office

Chapter Two
The Alamo Mission

The Alamo was originally named "Mission San Antonio de Valero" - a Spanish mission built in Texas for education of local American Indians after they converted to Christianity.

After the mission changed from religious to public, in 1793, it was abandoned. After 10 years, it became a fortress of San Carlos de Parras' military unit, who likely gave it the name of the Alamo.

In December 1835, General Martin Perfecto de Cos surrendered the fort to the Texian Army, following the siege of Bexar. A small number of Texian soldiers occupied the Alamo for several months.

The defenders were wiped out during the Battle of the Alamo, on March 6, 1836. When the Mexican Army retreated from Texas months later, they tore down many of the Alamo walls and burned some of the buildings. Periodically, the Alamo was used to house Texian and Mexican soldiers for the next 5 years but later was abandoned.

After Texas annexed to the United States, in 1849, the U.S. Army began renting the Alamo to use as a quartermasters depot but, then again, was abandoned, in 1876, after Fort Sam Houston was established. The Alamo chapel was sold to the state of Texas and tours were conducted but no renovations were done. The remaining buildings were sold to mercantiles and were used as wholesale grocery stores.

In 1891, "The Daughters of the Republic of Texas" was formed and started trying to preserve the Alamo. They convinced the state legislature, in 1905, to purchase the remaining buildings; the DRT was named as the permanent custodian of the Alamo.

In 2015, the Texas General Land Office was put in control of the Alamo by the Texas Land Commissioner. On July 5, 2015, the Alamo and the four missions were designated a "UNESCO World Heritage Site."

History

In 1716, several Roman Catholic missions were established by the Spanish government and the nearest settlement was 400 miles away. To assist the missionaries with provisions, the new governor of Spanish Texas wished to establish way stations between settlements along the Rio Grande.

Governor Martin de Alarcon led an expedition to find a new community in Texas, in April of 1718. They erected a temporary, new mission made of mud and straw. They built the mission near the head waters of the San Antonio River. Later, Alarcon built a fort - The Presidio San Antonio de Bexar. Alarcon founded the first community in Texas, San Antonio de Bexar, which later became San Antonio, Texas. In the next year, the mission was moved to the western bank of the river. Over a few years, several missions were established nearby.

In 1724, a Gulf Coast hurricane destroyed the

structures of the mission and this mission was moved to the current location. Over time, the mission expanded over three acres. The first to be built was L-shaped and 2-stories to house the priest. Other adobe buildings were for the missions Indians and workshops. The mission houses over 300 Indians and was self-sufficient for food and clothing.

In 1744, stones were laid for a permanent church but the church and tower collapsed in the late 1750s. In 1758, reconstruction started with the church being moved to the south end of the courtyard. The plans for the church intended to be 3-stories with bell towers, a dome and traditional cross; only 2-stories were done and the church was never completed. It was unlikely ever used for services but was carved with niches on either side of the doors to hold statues. The church walls were 4 feet thick and the walls enclosing it were 480 feet long from north to south and 160 feet from east to west along with being 8 feet high and 2 feet deep. Up to 30 adobe buildings were constructed to serve as storerooms, workshops and homes for Indian residents. The mission was built to withstand attacks by the Apache and the Comanche. For additional protection, three cannons were added by the front gate in 1762. By 1793, a 1-pounder was placed by the convent.

The Indian population, at the mission, was as high as 328, in 1756, to as low as 44, in 1777. The new Commandment General of the Provinces, Teodoro de Croix, ruled that all cattle, with no brand, belonged to the government. The mission's residents had a hard time rounding up the cattle and branding them because the Apache tribes were stealing the mission's horses.

The mission had lost a great deal of wealth because of the governments ruling and was unable to support the population of the converts. Only twelve Indians remained at the mission by 1793. Shortly after the mission was abandoned, most of the locals were not interested in the buildings. Visitors were impressed by the architecture.

Military

In the 19th century, the mission became known as the "Alamo." The name may have come from a nearby grove of cottonwood trees, known in Spanish as Alamo.

During the Mexican War of Independence, parts of the mission served as a political prison. San Antonio's first hospital was the mission.

After Mexico gained its independence, the buildings were transferred from Spanish to Mexican control, in 1821. Soldiers used the garrison until General Martin Perfecto de Cos surrendered to the Texan forces, in 1835.

The Battle of the Alamo

Date: February 23 - March 6, 1836

Location: Alamo Mission
San Antonio, Mexican Texas

Coordinates: 29°25'32"N 98°29'10"W

Result: Mexican victory

Belligerents: Mexican Republic | Republic of Texas

Commanders and Leaders:
Antonio Lopez de Santa Anna | William Travis
Manuel Fernandez Castrillon | James Bowie
Martin Perfecto de Cos | Davy Crockett
| William Carey
| George Kimble
| Almaron Dickinson

Strength: ~2,000 - 2,100 | 185 - 260

Casualties and Losses:
400 - 600 killed and wounded | 182 - 257 killed

Chapter Three
The Battle of the Alamo

On February 23, residents of Bexar were fleeing with the fear of Santa Anna's arrival, although Travis was still unconvinced of the reports, he stationed a soldier in the San Fernando Church Tower. The tower was the highest location in town for him to watch for signs of approaching forces.

Travis also sent Captain Philip Dimmitt and Lieutenant Benjamin Noble to look for the Mexican Army's location. That afternoon, the soldier rang the church bell stating he thought he had seen a flash in the distance. Since Dimmitt and Noble had not returned, Travis sent Dr. James Sutherland and John W. Smith to scout the area where they found the Mexican Cavalry as close as 1.5 miles from town. At the time, there were approximately 156 soldiers in the Alamo and another 14 in the hospital. The men scrounged for food from nearby homes and herded cattle into the garrison. They could only find enough food for about a month's time. A few of the men brought their families into the Alamo for safety. One of these was Almaron who brought his wife, Susannah, and their infant daughter, Angelina. Bowie brought in his deceased wife's cousin, Gertrudis Navarro, and Juana Navarro Alsbury and his son. He also brought Gregorio Esparza. His family climbed through the

Alamo's chapel window after Santa Anna's army arrived. Some of the garrison's members didn't report to duty because they didn't want to sneak by the Mexicans.

Earlier, as Santa Anna approached, Travis also sent John Johnson to ask Colonel Fannin, who was 100 miles southeast, to send reinforcements. Travis also sent Smith and Sutherland to take a message to the Major at Gonzales. The message read: "The enemy in large force is in sight. We want men and provisions, send them to us. We have 150 men and are determined to defend the Alamo to the last."

The Co-Commanders of the Alamo, William Travis and James Bowie, did not credit warnings that Santa Anna was coming and did not lay in food, supplies or ammunition. On February 23, they were surprised when Santa Anna arrived with his advanced detachment, an estimate of perhaps 1,800 men to as many as 6,000. His demand for unconditional surrender was answered with a cannon. This angered Santa Anna and he gave orders that no quarter was to be given… a 13 day siege began. The Mexican forces set up artillery positions opposite the south and east walls and then began a steady bombardment.

Santa Anna's Infantry maneuvered closer to the Alamo but stayed out of range of the Texans' rifled muskets.

The Mexicans who raised a blood red flag, meaning "No Quarter" and a Mexican bugler sounded with request for parley. Travis ordered the Alamo's cannon fired. The Mexicans fired back with 7-in Howitzers. The Mexicans firing caused no damage or injuries but the Alamo's firing killed 2 and injured 8 others.

Bowie thought Travis shouldn't have fired the cannon so he sent Green B. Jameson to meet with Santa Anna with a message addressed to the "Commander of the Invading Force of Bexar" and signed it "Commander of the Volunteers of Bexar."

The Mexican General was angry that Bowie presented himself equal to Santa Anna so, he refused to meet with Jameson. The Mexican General later allowed Colonel Juan Almonte and Jose Bartres to parley. Later, Almonte had said Jameson asked for an honorable surrender but Bartres replied that, "By order of his Excellency, we cannot come to terms with rebellious foreigners - if they wish to save their lives, than place themselves at the disposal of the Supreme Government." Travis was angry that Bowie took it upon himself to send Jameson to meet with Santa Anna. Bowie and Travis mutually agreed to fire the cannon again.

Nightfall took over and the firing ceased. By the time the parley was over, the Mexican's erected an artillery battery near the Veramendi House. That evening, Santa Anna sent General Ventura Mora's Calvary to circle the north and east of the Alamo so to prevent any reinforcements for Texians to arrive. A small part of Texians went out that evening and brought back 6 pack mules and a prisoner who would later be used to interpret Mexican bugle calls. That evening, when one of Seguin's men, Gregorio Esparza, arrived with his family, they had to be helped to climb through the chapel window to get in. Several other Texian soldiers couldn't make it back to the Alamo. Dimmitt and Noble, who were scouting, were told by the locals that Bexar was surrounded and they wouldn't be able to reenter the town. Andrew Jackson

Sowell and Byrd Lockhart were out looking for provisions that morning; on hearing that the Alamo was surrounded, they went back home to Gonzales.

February 24th

On Wednesday, February 24, was the first full day of the siege. The Mexican Army observed the Alamo's defense throughout the day. Santa Anna accompanied the cavalry on a scouting mission which came within musket range of the Alamo. Later that afternoon, Santa Anna ordered the Mexican artillery battery, consisting of 2 81B cannons and a mortar, to locate 350 yards from the Alamo to begin firing. Colonel Juan Almonte wrote in his diary that 2 of the Alamo's guns were dismounted but the Texians were able to bring them back into service quickly.

Bowie was confined to bed because he was feeling ill and had collapsed. He moved to a small room in the lower barracks of the south wall of the mission because of fear of him being contagious. Travis was now the sole Commander of the garrison. That afternoon, he wrote a letter and addressed it to the people of Texas and all Americans in the world; Travis sent the letter with Albert Martin, a courier who delivered it to Gonzales. In Gonzales, Lancelot Smithers took the message and delivered it to San Felipe where it was read by the Governor, Henry Smith. Smith told the people at San Felipe to "Go to the aid of your besieged countrymen and not let them be massacred by a mercenary foe." The call is to all who are able to bear arms and to go without one moment's delay or within 15 days. The heart of Texas will be the seat of the war.

Early that evening, Mexican Colonel Juan Bringas had led his scouts across a bridge over the San Antonio River. The Texian sharpshooters had killed one soldier and Davy Crockett had dropped another one as they were retreating. All through the night the Mexican Army bombarded the Alamo. They also were firing their muskets and shouted to make the Texians believe they either an assault was on the way or they were slaughtering the Texians' reinforcements. The Mexican soldiers used the darkness and the distractions of the Texians to station 2 more artillery batteries around the Alamo.

One of the batteries was located about 1,000 feet from the south wall of the Alamo; the other battery was located about 1,000 feet from the eastern wall of the Alamo.

By the end of the first day of fighting, Santa Anna's army had been reinforced by 600 of Sesma's troops.

February 25

The Mexican Army continued to bombard the Alamo through the morning of February 25. Early that morning, about 90 to 100 yards away from the Alamo, 200 to 300 Mexican soldiers took cover in abandoned shacks. The Texians thought the Mexican soldiers were planning an assault, but they intended to erect another artillery battery. Charles Despallier, Robert Brown, James Rose and a few others volunteered to burn the shacks even through it was broad daylight and in musket range of the Mexican soldiers. To provide cover, Dickinson and his men fired 8lb. cannons at the shacks while Crockett and his men fired their rifles. As soon as the Texians saw the shacks were inflamed, they opened the gates to the Alamo so the men could return, although Rose was almost captured by a Mexican officer. After six Mexican's were killed and four were wounded, they retreated. Santa Anna sent a messenger to tell Gaona to go to Bexar with his three best companies. In the meantime, Travis wrote another letter requesting help. Juan Seguin was voted in to go, by the Texian officers. Travis was adamant about Seguin not going because his knowledge of the language was invaluable along with the Mexican customs. Travis was told by his officers that because of Seguin's knowledge of the customs and language, it would help him get through. Seguin rode Bowie's horse because he was the fastest in the mission. Seguin didn't expect to survive this mission; he encountered American Calvary Patrol but, with his knowledge of Spanish and terrain, he escaped.

Despite the Texians burning down more of the shacks, the Mexican Army had setup an additional battery at a location known as the Powder House, approximately 1,000 yards from southeast of the Alamo. The Mexican Army now had artillery stationed on three sides of the Alamo.

February 26-27

Colonel Juan Bringas to engage the Texans. According to Ed Manson, one Texan was lost.

On February 26, Governor James W. Robinson had received word of the siege and immediately sent a courier to find Sam Houston.

Couriers were sent to other settlements. Reinforcements were gathering in Gonzales and were waiting for Fannin to arrive with more troops so they could travel together.

On the morning of February 26, Colonel James Fannin set out for a 90 mile trip to the Alamo with 320 men, 4 cannons and several supply wagons. Coming from Goliad, where the garrison had no horses, he had to rely on using oxen for the trip from Goliad to the Alamo. Within 200 yards, a wagon broke down and he had to stop for repairs. By the time they made repairs, it took 6 horses to cross the San Antonio River; it was dark by the time they reached the other side. The cold front reached Goliad and the men, poorly dressed, were miserable in the driving rain.

It took the Texans nearly the whole day to locate the oxen that wandered off and Fannin realized the men did not pack enough supplies for the journey.

It took two days for the Texians to travel one mile from their fort. Fannin wrote a letter to the acting Governor, James Robinson, stating that his officers had asked him to cancel the rescue trip. Because they received word that General Urrea's army was approaching Goliad, the officers and men claimed Fannin had aborted the mission on his own. In Dr. Bernard's writings in his journal, it was stated that several of the men agreed with the decision. With three to four hundred men, mostly on foot, low on saddles and marching nearly one hundred miles to relieve a fortress surrounded by five thousand men, was madness.

Fannin had sent a courier to Gonzales to tell Williamson to meet him at Cibolo Creek, which is halfway between Gonzales and San Antonio. Captain Albert Martin and about 60 men, on February 28, traveled 20 miles to meet Fannin at Cibolo Creek. Lindley speculates that Fannin had sent a relief force to scout the area around Bexar, headed up by Captain John

Chenoweth and Francis de Sauque. The advance force only reached as far as the Sequin Ranch to gather supplies, then turned back to Cibolo Creek to wait on Fannin and his men. Fannin had been seen marching from Goliad by several people that warned Santa Anna that he had 300 men with him; Colonel Juan Almonte and 800 men were ordered to intercept Fannin and his relief force.

Travis was unaware of Fannin's relief mission and had sent James Bonham to ask him for help. Bonham was told to wear a white kerchief around his hat so they would know it was him returning.

Santa Anna was low on supplies because his suppliers were in the rear convoy located with Goana and Filisola. Santa Anna wanted to restock in Bexar, but couldn't find much. He asked a local resident where to find provisions - Menchaca was a resident who led Santa Anna's army to the Seguin and Flores Ranches where he stole all their corn and livestock.

While the Mexican Army was trying to block the irrigation ditch leading to the Alamo, Green Jameson was trying to get the men to finish digging the well at the south end of the plaza. They hit water but the ground started giving way and the timber of the lower barracks collapsed.

On February 27, Martin and George Kimball, and 25 men, set out from Gonzales after learning Fannin wasn't coming.

February 28 - March 2

One of the volunteer's, John G. King, fifteen year old son asked if he could take his father's place because his father was needed to take care of his family's nine children. The men agreed he could and William traded places with his father. Eight additional men joined them as they marched to Bexar.

The men carried the first flag ever made to use in a Texian battle, "The Come and Take It Flag" from the Battle of Gonzales.

According to Lindley, Martin and Smith and approximately 34 other men, chose to not wait for Fannin and continued to Bexar.

On February 29, Colonel Wharton was preparing to cross the Guadalupe River, while in San Felipe, Captain Mosley Baker ordered the local militia to prepare to march. Meanwhile, Seguin recruited 25 men and Dr. Sutherland and Horace Asbury recruited 12 more men. They all set out for Cibolo in hope of meeting Fannin on February 28.

While all this was happening, Bonham spoke with Fannin, who again declined to relieve the Alamo. A nineteen year old, Ben Highsmith, who had left the Alamo as a courier before Santa Anna arrived, tried to go back to the Alamo but was chased 6 miles by the Mexican Army. He met Bonham in Gonzales and told him that no one could get through Mexican lines. Bonham did not take the warning and on March 2, crossed the Guadalupe headed to the Alamo.

Unbeknownst to the Mexican and Texian soldiers, on March 2, the delegates to the Convention of 1836 adopted the "Texas Declaration of Independence."

Now the Texians were fighting for the Republic of Texas. On the evening of March 2, the Convention finally received Travis' letter of February 25. The delegates took no action because they had received word that Fannin had left Goliad for the Alamo and thought the Alamo would be adequately reinforced.

During this time, the Mexican Army had a battalion set up on the east side of the complex and a second battalion set up on the left guarding the road to Gonzales. Santa Anna, himself, conducted a scouting trip and discovered a road near the Alamo and moved the second battalion to guard it. On March 3, Bonham made it to Bexar wearing a white bandana on his hat to let the Texians know he was one of them. He sped through the Mexican Army and made it through the gate unharmed. Bonham broke the news, to the garrison, that Fannin would not be coming. Travis sent a courier to the Convention notifying them that, so far, they had survived the siege and now only depended on the aid of the colonies. If no help arrives, Travis said he would have to fight on his own terms and do the best they can and he will not fail his men on the last struggle. Although they may be sacrificed to the vengeance of the enemy, the victory will cost the enemy dear... that will be worse than defeat. Travis said they would fire the cannon three times each day to show they still held the fort. According to Lindley's research, 50 of Fannin's men, on March 3, likely joined Chenoweth's and DeSauque's advanced group as well as Seguin and his unit. The entire group joined a group waiting at Cibolo Creek, 35 miles from the Alamo.

After marching for days, the Zapadoes, Aldama and Toluca Battalions arrived to reinforce Santa Anna. The Texians watched from the wall as approximately 1,000 Mexican troops, in dress uniform, marched into Bexar's military plaza. The Mexican Army celebrated the news of troops, under General Jose de Urrea, defeating Texian Colonel Frank W. Johnson at the Battle of San Patricia, on February 27.

The number of Mexican soldiers located in Bexar was brought to approximately 2,400. The bombardments from the Mexican battery impacting the walls was causing the walls to crumble. By nightfall, the walls were beginning to collapse and the men kept working all night to shear them up with boards.

In 1876, Susannah Dickinson said that Travis had sent out three men after dark. The three men, who Dickinson believed included Davy Crockett, were to go find Fannin. Lindley stated Crockett and another man found the Texian force waiting along Cibolo Creek. On March 4, part of the Texians broke through to the Alamo. The second group was driven across the prairie by Mexican soldiers.

Lindley based his reports on 2 newspaper reports, within a month on the fall of the Alamo, that stated 50 men had reinforced the Alamo.

On March 4, Santa Anna called on his Council of War and proposed an imminent attack on the Alamo. Many of his officers disagreed because they wanted to wait on heavy artillery. They were waiting on two, 12-1B cannons with capability of knocking down the Alamo walls. They were due to arrive on March 7. According to reports by Filisola, on March 4, a woman from Bexar was informing Santa Anna that Travis and his men were going to either surrender or escape if they didn't receive reinforcements. Years later, Dickinson believed Juana Alsbury left the fort that evening believing that she deserted to provide information about the Texian troops strength to Santa Anna. Edmenson notes that Alsbury came back to the Alamo and speculates that Travis sent her to try to negotiate a surrender for the Texian troops. According to Todish, more than one historian and some of Santa Anna's officers, it was speculated this was why Santa Anna pushed for an immediate assault rather Han wait for the heavy guns.

On March 5, Santa Anna called another staff meeting and announced that the assault would commence on the following day. The officers still insisted on waiting for the heavy guns. According to his aide, Fernando Ur Issa, Santa Anna said, "What are lives of soldiers than so many chickens?"

He said, "The Alamo must fall and my orders must be obeyed."

General Valentin Amador drew up the detailed battle orders: all soldiers to wear shoes or sandals, properly tie chin straps, do not wear cloaks or blankets - each soldier to receive 4 to 6 rounds of ammunition and to be given two flints.

The Mexican soldiers were divided and placed into four columns. The first column was commanded by Cos; the second column was commanded by Colonel Francisco Duque; the third column was commanded by Colonel Jose Maria Romero and the fourth column was commanded by Juan Morales.

Santa Anna commanded the reserve force. The calvary would patrol and guard the camp.

On March 5, Travis gathered the men and explained that it was likely an attack would take place and, that evening, one last courier, James Allen, was sent out with messages from Travis and some of the men.

Travis, at the time, asked of those who were willing to die for the Texian cause… to cross the line and stand next to him.

Bowie, who was bedridden, asked Crockett and other men to carry his bed across the line. That left only one man left on the other side of the line - Louis "Moses" Rose - who said he wasn't ready to die; he escaped that evening. A reporter wrote this article 35 years after the Alamo fell, stating his parents heard the story directly from Rose himself. The reporter admitted he embellished pieces of the article and that Rose had died before the came out so the story couldn't be authenticated. Years after the story came out, two of the Alamo survivors, Susannah Dickinson and Enrique Esparza, had some conflicting details of the incident.

The Mexican artillery ceased their bombardment at 10:00 PM and, as Santa Anna had planned, the Texians fell to sleep because they hadn't had any rest since the siege began. There were only three sentries outside the wall.

March 6

At midnight, Santa Anna moved his soldiers quietly into place, being ready for the battle. As they moved into place, they surprised and killed the three sentries that were on guard. Although Santa Anna gave the starting time to be at 4:00 AM, his soldiers did not get all of them in place until 5:00 AM.

The Mexican Army got within 300 feet of the Alamo and, at 5:30 AM, Santa Anna gave the order to advance. His troops, being excited, began shouting, "Viva Santa Anna, Viva la Republic…" they messed up and woke up the Texians.

By the time the Texians reached their post, the Mexicans were already in musket range. Cos and his men advanced towards the northwest corner of the Alamo. Duque led his men towards a repaired breach in the north wall, from the northwest. Romero advanced toward the east wall and Morales's men advanced towards the lower parapet, by the chapel.

Travis rushed out yelling, "Come on, boys! The Mexicans are upon us; we'll give them hell!"

Cos had 350 troops with 10 ladders, 2 crowbars and 2 axes. Duque had 400 men and 10 ladders. Romero had 400 men and 6 ladders. Morales had 125 men and 2 ladders. Sesma had 500 calvary and Santa Anna had 400 reserve.

At the beginning, the Mexicans had a disadvantage - being in columns, only the front row could fire their muskets. Having untrained troops, some of the recruits in the back ranks fired their muskets, killing or injuring the troops in front of them.

The Mexican troops, being so tightly together, made excellent targets for the Texians. The Texians, not having enough shot, loaded their cannons with any metal they could find, such as, chopped up horse shoes, nails, door hinges - essentially turning the cannons into giant shotguns.

While the Mexican soldiers pushed each other up against the walls, the Texians had to lean over the wall to fire at the attacker; this exposed them into the open to Mexican fire. Travis was one of the first to die while firing his shotgun into the Mexican soldiers below. It was told, by one source, that he drew his sword and killed a Mexican officer before he died. Most Mexican soldiers using ladders to scale the walls were either shot or beaten back but the Texians found it hard to reload the muskets as the Mexicans came over the walls.

The Mexican Army withdrew and regrouped for a second and third attack. During the third attack, the Mexican soldiers closest to the north wall found that the makeshift wall had gaps and toeholds to help scale the 12 foot wall. The first to scale the wall was Colonel Juan Amador; his men saw this and began swarming the wall, allowing them to pour into the complex. The Texians at the south wall turned their cannon around towards the north, firing into the advancing Mexican soldiers. Meanwhile, it left the south wall unprotected and within minutes, the Mexican soldiers had scaled the wall and killed the gunners. The Mexican soldiers had captured the Texians 181B cannon. At that time, Romero's men had taken over the east wall and poured into the complex.

The Texians fell back to the barracks and the chapel. The Texians, stationed at the west wall were unable to reach the barracks, headed toward the San Antonio River and took cover at the ditch while the calvary was charging. Sesma sent reinforcements and eventually the Texians were killed. The Texians that were at the cattle pens scrambled over the lower wall after discharging their weapons. They circled behind the church and raced on foot into the east prairie and the Mexican calvary advanced on the group. Almaron Dickinson and his artillery crew turned their cannon around and fired into the calvary, but all the escaping Texians were eventually killed.

Crockett and his men were the last Texian group defending the lower wall in front of the church. Unable to reload, they used the rifles as clubs and fought with their knives. After the Mexicans firing and using their bayonets, the last few Texians remaining moved back to the church. The church and the rooms along the east and west walls were the only places unoccupied by the Mexican Army. The Mexican soldiers saw the Texian's flag waving from the top of one of the buildings; four Mexican soldiers were killed before the flag of Mexico was raised. Many of the remaining Texians were in the fortified barrack's rooms. The Texians had neglected to spike the cannon before retreating. The Mexicans used the cannon to blow the doors off the barracks, then fired into the barracks before running in to take over.

Bowie, being too sick to fight, was likely killed in his bed. Witnesses gave conflicting accounts of his death. Some say they saw Mexican soldiers going into his room, bayonet him, then carry him out alive. Others say he shot himself or was killed by soldiers. According to Historian Wallace Charlton, the most popular and probably the most accurate depiction was that he died with his back against the wall, fighting with both his pistols and his famous knife.

11 men manning the 121B cannon in the chapel were the last to die. The Mexicans fired the 181B cannon and destroyed the barricades. As they entered the building, the crew fired their 121B cannon into the Mexicans coming through the door.

They had no time to reload so, they grabbed their rifles and fired before they were bayonetted to death. Among them were Dickinson, Gregorio, Esparza and James Bonham. Texian Robert Evans had been tasked to keep the gunpowder from falling into the hands of the Mexicans; wounded, he crawled with a torch inches from the gunpowder and was killed by a musket ball. If he would have succeeded, the blast would have killed them women and children hiding in the sacristy of the church.

As the soldiers approached the sacristy, a young boy, the son of one of the occupiers, Anthony Wolf, stood up and put a blanket over his shoulders. One of the Mexican soldiers mistook him for an adult and killed him. Possibly one of the last persons to die was Jacob Walker; he was trying to hide behind Susannah Dickinson and was bayonetted in front of the woman. Brigido Guerrero also sought refuge in the sacristy. He deserted the Mexican Army, in December 1835, but was spared by convincing the Mexican soldiers he was held captive by the Texians.

The battle for the Alamo was over by 6:30 AM. Mexican soldiers were inspecting the bodies and bayonetting any that moved. Even with all the Texians dead, the Mexican soldiers kept shooting and killing each other in the confusion. The Mexican generals were unable to stop it and appealed to Santa Anna for help. Even when Santa Anna showed himself, it wouldn't stop until the bugle was blown for retreat.

A former United States slave, Ben - a cook for one of Santa Anna's officers, maintained that Crockett's body was found surrounded by no less than 16 Mexican corpses. Historians disagree on which version of Crockett's death was accurate.

Santa Anna's initial report claimed there were 600 Texians killed and 70 Mexican soldiers killed and 300 wounded. His secretary stated 400 killed. Other estimates of Mexican soldiers went from 60 to 200 with 250 to 300 wounded. Some historians and survivors, like Susannah Dickinson, estimated that over 1,000 to 1,600 Mexican soldiers were killed or wounded, but most likely, the casualties were less than 600.

Mexican soldiers were buried in the local cemetery, Camp Santo, shortly after the battle.

The Texian bodies were stacked and burned. The only exception was Gregorio Esparza because his brother, Francisco, was an officer in Santa Anna's army and was given permission to give him a proper burial.

The ashes of the Texians were left where they fell. Juan Seguin returned to Bexar, in February 1837, to examine the remains - a simple coffin with the names, Travis, Crockett and Bowie, inscribed on it. It was filled with ashes from the funeral pyres. According to an article in the *Telegraph and Texas Register*, Seguin buried the coffin under a peach tree grove but the spot was never marked and now cannot be identified. Seguin later claimed that he placed the coffin in front of the altar at the San Fernando Cathedral.

Santa Anna spared Travis' slave, Joe, in an attempt to convince other slaves in Texas to support the Mexican Government.

Santa Anna was impressed by Susannah Dickinson and offered to adopt her daughter and educate her in Mexico City… Dickinson refused his offer.

Each woman was given a blanket and 2 silver pesos. Alsbury and other Tejano women were allowed to return to their home in Bexar.

Dickinson and her daughter were sent to Gonzales, escorted by Joe and was to relate the events of the battle and to tell the rest of the Texian forces that Santa Anna's army is unbeatable.

Chapter Four
Excerpts and List of Defenders

Excerpt from William B. Travis' letter to the people of Texas and all the Americans in the world:

"I am determined to sustain myself as long as possible and die like a soldier who never forgets what is due to his own honor and that of his country."

"Victory or Death"

Last words of Texian defender Almaron Dickinson, to his wife Susannah, as he prepared to defend the chapel:

"Great God, Sue, the Mexicans are inside our walls! If they spare you, save my child."

Defenders

(Listed in order of name, rank, birth year, birthplace, status, legacy & notes, ref(s))

- Juan Abarnillo, SGT, —, Texas, fatality, Entered March 4

- James L. Allen, PVT, 1815, Kentucky, survivor, Left on March 5 as the final courier sent from the Alamo
- Robert Allen, PVT, —, Virginia, fatality
- Horace Alsbury, PVT, 1805, Kentucky, survivor, First courier sent out after the arrival of Mexican troops on February 23
- George Andrews, —, —, —, fatality, Entered March 4
- Miles DeForest Andross, PVT, 1809, Vermont, fatality
- José Maria Arocha, —, —, —, survivor, Juan Seguin's volunteers
- Simon Arreola, —, —, —, survivor, Juan Seguin's volunteers
- Micajah Autry, PVT, 1793 [34], North Carolina, fatality
- Jesse B. Badgett, —, 1807, North Carolina, survivor, Garrison delegate to the March 1 Convention of 1836, at Washington-on-the-Brazos
- Juan A. Badillo, SGT, —, Texas, fatality, Entered March 4
- Peter James Bailey III, PVT, 1812, Kentucky, fatality, Namesake of Bailey County, Texas
- Isaac G. Baker, PVT, 1814, Arkansas, fatality, Gonzales Mounted Ranger Company
- William Charles M. Baker, CPT, —, Missouri, fatality
- John Ballard, —, —, —, fatality, Gonzales Mounted Ranger Company
- John J. Ballentine, PVT, —, Pennsylvania, fatality
- Richard W. Ballentine, PVT, 1814, Scotland, fatality
- Andrew Barcena, —, —, —, survivor

- John J. Baugh, CPT, 1803, Virginia, fatality, Adjutant of the garrison, next in command after co-commanders Bowie and Travis
- Samuel G. Bastian, —, —, Louisiana, survivor, Left February 29 as a courier to Gonzales, unable to enter the Alamo
- Joseph Bayliss, PVT, 1808, Tennessee, fatality
- John Walker Baylor Jr., PVT, 1813, Kentucky, survivor, Sent as a courier to Goliad
- Anselmo Bergara, —, —, Mexico, survivor
- John Blair, PVT, 1803, Tennessee, fatality
- Samuel Blair, CPT, 1807, Tennessee, fatality, Assistant to Master of Ordnance
- William Blazeby, CPT, 1795, England, fatality
- James Bonham, 2LT, 1807, South Carolina, fatality, Courier to Goliad and Gonzales, returned March 3, possibly died manning one of the cannons
- Daniel Bourne, PVT, 1810, England, fatality
- James Bowie, COL, c. 1796, Kentucky, fatality, Co-commander of the garrison after the departure of James C. Neill
- J. B. Bowman, —, —, —, fatality, Possibly a.k.a. James H. Bowman
- Robert Brown, PVT, c. 1818, —, survivor, Left after February 25, later served as a baggage guard at the Battle of San Jacinto
- James Buchanan, PVT, 1813, Alabama, fatality
- Samuel E. Burns, PVT, 1810, Ireland, fatality
- George D. Butler, PVT, 1813, Missouri Territory, fatality
- John Cain, PVT, 1802, Pennsylvania, fatality, Gonzales Mounted Ranger Company
- Robert Campbell, LT, 1810, Tennessee, fatality

- William R. Carey, CPT, 1806, Virginia, fatality
- Cesario Carmona, —, —, —, survivor, Juan Seguin's volunteer
- M. B. Clark, PVT, —, Mississippi, fatality, Entered March 4
- Daniel W. Cloud, PVT, 1812, Kentucky, fatality
- Robert E. Cochran, PVT, 1810, New Hampshire, fatality, Namesake of Cochran County, Texas
- George Washington Cottle, LT, 1811, Missouri, fatality, Entered March 1 or 4 Gonzales Mounted Ranger Company; namesake of Cottle County, Texas
- Henry Courtman, PVT, 1808, Germany, fatality, Entered March 4
- Lemuel Crawford, PVT, 1814, South Carolina, fatality
- David Crockett, COL, 1786, Tennessee, fatality, Frontiersman and congressman, his life was portrayed in many exploits during and after his death
- Robert Crossman, PVT, 1810, Pennsylvania, fatality
- Antonio Cruz y Arocha, PVT, —, Mexico, survivor, Left as courier with Seguin on February 25
- David P. Cummings, PVT, 1809, Pennsylvania, fatality, Gonzales Mounted Ranger Company
- Robert Cunningham, PVT, 1804, New York, fatality
- Matias Curvier, —, —, —, survivor, Juan Seguin's volunteers
- Jacob C. Darst, LT, 1793, Kentucky, fatality, Entered March 1 or 4 Gonzales Mounted Ranger Company
- John Davis, PVT, 1811, Kentucky, fatality, Gonzales Mounted Ranger Company

- Freeman H.K. Day, PVT, 1806, —, fatality, Entered March 1 or 4
- Squire Daymon, PVT, 1808, Tennessee, fatality, Gonzales Mounted Ranger Company
- William Dearduff, PVT, c. 1811, Tennessee, fatality, Gonzales Mounted Ranger Company
- Alexandro De la Garza, PVT, —, Texas, survivor, Dispatched as a courier
- Stephen Dennison, PVT, 1812, England or Ireland, fatality, Entered March 4
- Francis L. DeSauque, CPT, —, Pennsylvania, survivor, Left to gather supplied at Goliad
- John Desauque, —, —, Louisiana, fatality, Salve of Desauque, served as a combatant (Slaves identified by last names of their masters)
- Charles Despallier, PVT, 1812, Louisiana, fatality, Gonzales Mounted Ranger Company
- Lewis Dewall, PVT, 1812, New York, fatality
- Almaron Dickinson, CPT, 1810, Tennessee, fatality
- James Dickson, —, —, —, fatality, —
- John Henry Dillard, PVT, 1805, Tennessee, fatality
- Philip Dimmitt, CPT, 1801, Kentucky, survivor, On a scouting run when the Mexican troops arrived on February 23
- James R. Dimpkins, SGT, —, England, fatality
- Andrew Duvalt, PVT, 1804, Ireland, fatality, Gonzales Mounted Ranger Company
- Samuel M. Edwards, —, —, —, fatality, Entered March 4
- Conrad Eigenauer, —, —, —, fatality, Entered March 4
- J. D. Elliott, —, —, —, fatality, Entered March 4
- Frederick E. Elms, —, —, —, fatality, Gonzales Mounted Ranger Company

- Lucio Enriques, —, —, —, survivor, Juan Seguin's volunteers
- Carlos Espalier, PVT, 1819, Texas, fatality, Entered March 4
- José Gregorio Esparza, PVT, 1802, Texas, fatality
- Robert Evans, MAJ, 1800, Ireland, fatality, Master of Ordnance
- Samuel B. Evans, PVT, 1812, New York, fatality
- James L. Ewing, PVT, 1812, Tennessee, fatality
- William Keener Fauntleroy, PVT, 1814, Kentucky, fatality
- William Fishbaugh, PVT, —, Alabama, fatality, Gonzales Mounted Ranger Company
- John Flanders, PVT, 1800, Salisbury, Massachusetts, fatality, Gonzales Mounted Ranger Company
- Manuel N. Flores, —, c. 1801, Texas, survivor, Juan Seguin's volunteers
- Salvador Flores, CPT, 1806, Texas, survivor, Left with Seguin on February 25
- Dolphin Ward Floyd, PVT, 1804, North Carolina, fatality, Namesake of Floyd County, Texas; Gonzales Mounted Ranger Company
- John Hubbard Forsyth, CPT, 1797, New York, fatality
- Antonio Fuentes, PVT, 1813, Texas, fatality
- Galba Fuque, PVT, 1819, Alabama, fatality, Entered March 1 or 4 Gonzales Mounted Ranger Company
- William Garnett, PVT, 1812, Virginia, fatality
- James W. Garland, PVT, 1813, Louisiana, fatality
- James Girard Garrett, PVT, 1806, Tennessee, fatality

- John E. Garvin, PVT, 1809, —, fatality, Gonzales Mounted Ranger Company
- John E. Gaston, PVT, 1819, —, fatality, Entered March 1 or 4 Gonzales Mounted Ranger Company
- James George, PVT, 1802, —, fatality, Entered March 1 or 4 Gonzales Mounted Ranger Company
- William George, —, —, —, fatality, Entered March 1 or 4
- James Gibson, —, —, —, fatality, Gonzales Mounted Ranger Company
- John C. Goodrich, CNT, 1809, Virginia, fatality
- Francis H. Gray, —, —, —, fatality, Entered March 4
- W. T. Green, —, —, —, fatality, Entered March 4
- Albert Calvin Grimes, PVT, 1817, Georgia, fatality
- Ignacio Gurrea, —, —, —, survivor, Juan Seguin's volunteers
- Brigido Guerrero, PVT, —, Mexico, survivor, A deserter from Ugartechea's troops, convinced the Mexican troops he was a prisoner of war
- James C. Gwin, PVT, 1804, England, fatality, aka Gwynne
- John Harris, PVT, 1813, Kentucky, fatality
- Andrew Jackson Harrison, PVT, 1809, Tennessee, fatality
- I. L. K. Harrison, —, —, —,, fatality
- William B. Harrison, CPT, 1811, Ohio, fatality
- Joseph M. Hawkins, PVT, 1799, Ireland, fatality
- John M. Hays, PVT, 1814, Tennessee, fatality
- Charles M. Heiskill, PVT, 1813, Tennessee, fatality
- Patrick Henry Herndon, PVT, 1802, Virginia, fatality
- Pedro Herrera, —, —, —, survivor, Juan Seguin's volunteers

- William Daniel Hersee, SGT, 1805, England, fatality
- Benjamin Franklin Highsmith, PVT, 1817, Missouri Territory, survivor, Left as a courier March 1
- Tapley Holland, PVT, 1810, Ohio, fatality, First to cross over the line in the sand
- James Holloway, —, —, —, fatality, Entered March 4
- Samuel Holloway, PVT, 1808, Pennsylvania, fatality
- William D. Howell, —, 1791, Massachusetts, fatality, Entered March 4
- William Hunter, —, —, —, fatality, Entered March 4
- Thomas P. Hutchinson, —, —, —, fatality, Entered March 4
- William A. Irwin, —, —, —, fatality, Gonzales Mounted Ranger Company,
- Thomas R. Jackson, PVT, —, Ireland, fatality, Entered March 1 or 4 Gonzales Mounted Ranger Company
- William Daniel Jackson, LT, 1807, Kentucky, fatality
- Green B. Jameson, MAJ, 1807, Kentucky, fatality
- Gordon C. Jennings, CPL, 1780, Connecticut, fatality, Oldest defender of the Alamo
- Damacio Jiménez, PVT, —, Texas, fatality, Entered March 4
- John Johnson, PVT, 1800, Missouri, survivor, Dispatched as courier February 23
- Lewis Johnson, PVT, —, Illinois Territory, fatality
- William Johnson, PVT —, Pennsylvania, fatality
- William P. Johnson, SGT, —, —, survivor, Likely dispatched as courier February 23
- John Jones, 1LT, 1810, New York, fatality

- John Benjamin Kellogg, LT, 1817, Kentucky, fatality, Resident of Gonzales, Texas. Joined relief force from Gonzales, arrived March 1, 1836.
- James Kenny, PVT, 1814, Virginia, fatality
- Andrew Kent, PVT, 1791, Kentucky, fatality, Namesake of Kent County, Texas, Gonzales Mounted Ranger Company
- Joseph Kent, —, —, —, fatality, Entered March 1 or 4 Gonzales Mounted Ranger Company
- Joseph Kerr, PVT, 1814, Louisiana, fatality
- George C. Kimble, LT, 1803, Pennsylvania, fatality, Namesake of Kimble County, Texas; entered March 1 or 4 Gonzales Mounted Ranger Company
- John C. Kin, —, —, —, fatality, Gonzales Mounted Ranger Company
- William Philip King, PVT, 1820, Mississippi, fatality, Youngest defender fatality; namesake of King County, Texas; Gonzales Mounted Ranger Company
- William Irvine Lewis, PVT, 1806, Virginia, fatality
- William J. Lightfoot, 3CPL, 1805, Kentucky, fatality
- Jonathan Lindley, PVT, 1814, Illinois, fatality, Gonzales Mounted Ranger Company
- William Linn, PVT, —, Massachusetts, fatality
- Byrd Lockhart, CPT, 1782, Virginia, survivor, Left with Andrew Jackson Sowell left to buy supplies; namesake of Lockhart, Texas
- Toribio Losoya, PVT, 1808, Texas, fatality
- George Washington Main, LT, 1807, Virginia, fatality
- William T. Malone, PVT, 1817, Georgia, fatality
- William Marshall, PVT, 1808, Tennessee, fatality

- Albert Martin, CPT, 1808, Rhode Island, fatality, Gonzales Mounted Ranger Company dispatched with the Travis letter To the People of Texas & All Americans in the World; returned to the Alamo
- Samuel Augustus Maverick, PVT, 1803, South Carolina, survivor, Garrison delegate to the March 1 Convention of 1836 at Washington-on-the-Brazos
- Edward McCafferty, LT, —, —, fatality, Entered March 4
- Ross McClelland, —, —, —, fatality
- Daniel McCoy Jr., —, —, —, fatality, Gonzales Mounted Ranger Company
- Jesse McCoy, PVT, 1804, Tennessee, fatality, Gonzales Mounted Ranger Company
- Prospect McCoy, —, —, —, fatality
- William McDowell, PVT, 1794, Pennsylvania, fatality
- James McGee, PVT, —, Ireland, fatality
- John McGregor, PVT, —, Scotland, fatality
- Robert McKinney, PVT, 1809, Ireland, fatality
- S. W. McNeilly, —, —, —, fatality, Entered March
- Eliel Melton, QM, LT, 1798, Georgia, fatality
- Antonio Menchaca, —, 1800, Texas, survivor, Juan Seguin's volunteers
- Thomas R. Miller, PVT, 1795, Tennessee, fatality, Gonzales Mounted Ranger Company
- William Mills, PVT, 1815, Tennessee, fatality
- Isaac Millsaps, PVT, c. 1795, Mississippi, fatality, Gonzales Mounted Ranger Company
- Edward F. Mitchasson, —, 1806, Virginia, fatality, Entered March 4 a.k.a. Dr. E.F. Mitchusson
- Edwin T. Mitchell, PVT, 1806, —, fatality, Entered March 4

- Napoleon B. Mitchell, PVT, 1804, —, fatality
- Robert B. Moore, PVT, 1781, Virginia, fatality, Entered March 4
- Willis A. Moore, PVT, 1808, Marion County, MS, fatality, Entered March 4
- John Morman, —, —, —, fatality
- William Morrison, —, —, —, fatality, Gonzales Mounted Ranger Company
- Robert Musselman, SGT, 1805, Ohio, fatality
- James Nash, —, —, —, fatality, Gonzales Mounted Ranger Company
- Andrés Nava, SGT, 1810, Texas, fatality, Entered March 4
- Gerald Navan, PVT, —, —, survivor, Dispatched as courier March 3
- George Neggan, PVT, 1808, South Carolina, fatality, Gonzales Mounted Ranger Company
- Andrew M. Nelson, PVT, 1809, Tennessee, fatality
- Edward Nelson, PVT, 1816, South Carolina, fatality
- George Nelson, PVT, 1805, South Carolina, fatality
- Benjamin F. Nobles, LT, —, —, survivor, On a scouting run when the Mexican troops arrived on February 23
- James Northcross, PVT, 1804, Virginia, fatality
- James Nowlan, PVT, 1809, England, fatality
- L. R. O'Neil, —, —, —, fatality, Entered March 4
- George Olamio, PVT, —, Ireland, fatality, Entered March 4
- William Sanders Oury, PVT, 1817, Virginia, survivor, Dispatched as a courier February 29
- Jose Sebastian "Luciano" Pacheco, —, —, —, survivor, Dispatched on a personal errand for Seguin February 23

- George Pagan, PVT, 1810, —, fatality
- Christopher Adams Parker, PVT, 1814, —, fatality
- William Parks, PVT, 1805, North Carolina, fatality
- William Patton, AQM, LT, 1808, Kentucky, fatality, survivor, Assumed to be a courier, who left with John William Smith
- Richardson Perry, PVT, 1817, Mississippi, fatality
- Amos Pollard, —, 1803, Massachusetts, fatality, Chief surgeon of the garrison, created a hospital in the fortress
- Eduardo Ramirez, —, —, —, survivor, Juan Seguin's volunteers
- John Purdy Reynolds, PVT, 1806, Pennsylvania, fatality
- Thomas H. Roberts, PVT, —, —, fatality, Entered March 4
- James Waters Robertson, PVT, 1812, Tennessee, fatality
- Ambrosio Rodriguez, —, —, —, survivor, Juan Seguin's volunteers
- Guadalupe Rodriguez, —, —, —, fatality, Entered March 4
- James M. Rose, PVT, 1805, Ohio, fatality, With Crockett; not to be confused with Louis Moses Rose, the individual purported to have chosen not to stay and defend the Alamo (but who cannot definitely be proven to have been there)
- Jacob Roth, MAJ, —, —, fatality
- Jackson J. Rusk, PVT, —, Ireland, fatality
- Joseph Rutherford, PVT, 1798, Kentucky, fatality
- Isaac Ryan, PVT, 1805, Louisiana, fatality
- W. H. Sanders, —, —, —, fatality, Entered March 4
- Mial Scurlock, PVT, 1809, North Carolina, fatality

- Juan Seguin, CPT, 1806, Texas, survivor, Left February 25 to recruit reinforcements
- Marcus L. Sewell, PVT, 1805, England, fatality, Gonzales Mounted Ranger Company
- Manson Shied, PVT, 1811, Georgia, fatality, aka Shudd
- Silvero, —, —, —, survivor, Juan Seguin's volunteers
- Cleveland Kinloch Simmons, LT, 1815, South Carolina, fatality, —
- Andrew H. Smith, PVT, 1815, Tennessee, fatality
- Charles S. Smith, PVT, 1806, Maryland, fatality
- John William Smith, —, 1792, Virginia, survivor, The final courier sent to Washington-on-the-Brazos, unable to return
- Joshua G. Smith, SGT, 1808, North Carolina, fatality
- William H. Smith, PVT, 1811, —, fatality
- Launcelot Smither, PVT, 1800, —, survivor, Left for Gonzales as a courier on February 23; relayed the Travis letter from Albert Martin to the provisional government at San Felipe
- Andrew Jackson Sowell, PVT, 1815, Tennessee, survivor, Left with Byrd Lockhart to buy supplies
- John Spratt, —, —, —, fatality, Entered March 4
- Richard Starr, PVT, 1811, England, fatality
- James E. Stewart, PVT, 1808, England, fatality
- Richard L. Stockton, PVT, 1817, New Jersey, fatality
- A. Spain Summerlin, PVT, 1817, Tennessee, fatality
- William E. Summers, PVT, 1812, South Carolina, fatality, Gonzales Mounted Ranger Company

- John Sutherland, PVT, 1792, Virginia, survivor, Sent to Gonzales for reinforcements February 23
- William DePriest Sutherland, PVT, 1818, Alabama, fatality
- Edward Taylor, PVT, 1812, Tennessee, fatality, Namesake of Taylor County, brother of James and George, entered March 1 or 4
- George Taylor, PVT, 1816, Tennessee, fatality, Namesake of Taylor County, brother of Edward and James, entered March 1 or 4
- James Taylor, PVT, 1814, Tennessee, fatality, Namesake of Taylor County, Texas, brother of George and Edward, entered March 1 or 4
- William Taylor, PVT, 1814, Tennessee, fatality, Entered March 1 or 4
- B. Archer M. Thomas, PVT, 1818, Kentucky, fatality
- Henry Thomas, PVT, 1811, Germany, fatality, Entered March 4
- Thompson, —, —, —, fatality, Per historian Lindley, no first name on the muster rolls
- John W. Thomson, PVT, 1807, North Carolina, fatality
- John M. Thurston, 2LT, 1812, Pennsylvania, fatality
- Burke Trammel, PVT, 1810, Ireland, fatality
- Joe Travis, —, 1813 or 1815, Alabama, survivor, Slave of William B. Travis, fought beside him in the battle; accompanied Susanna Dickinson to Gonzales. (Slaves identified by last name of their masters)
- William B. Travis, LTC, 1809, South Carolina, fatality, Co-commander of the garrison after the departure of James C. Neill

- George W. Tumlinson, PVT, 1814, Missouri Territory, fatality, Gonzales Mounted Ranger Company
- James Tylee, PVT, 1795, New York, fatality
- Asa Walker, PVT, 1813, Tennessee, fatality
- Jacob Walker, PVT, 1799, Tennessee, fatality
- William B. Ward, SGT, 1806, Ireland, fatality
- Henry Warnell, PVT, 1812, Arkansas, escaped, Died June 1836 of wounds incurred during the battle or during his escape
- Joseph G. Washington, PVT, c. 1808, Tennessee, fatality, Possibly a.k.a. James Morgan
- Thomas Waters, PVT, 1812, England, fatality
- William Wells, PVT, 1798, Georgia, fatality
- Isaac White, SGT, —, —, fatality
- Robert White, CPT, 1806, England, fatality, Gonzales Mounted Ranger Company
- Hiram James Williamson, SGM, 1810, Pennsylvania, fatality
- Williams Wills, —, —, —, fatality
- David L. Wilson, PVT, 1807, Scotland, fatality
- John Wilson, PVT, 1804, Pennsylvania, fatality
- Anthony Wolf, PVT, 1782. —, fatality
- Claiborne Wright, PVT, 1810, North Carolina, fatality, Gonzales Mounted Ranger Company
- Charles Zanco, LT, 1808, Denmark, fatality
- Vicente Zepeda, —, —, —, survivor, Juan Seguin's volunteers

Chapter Five
Battle of San Jacinto

After the siege of the Alamo, Santa Anna's Mexican forces were approaching; Houston and his troops, that were under his command, began to withdraw to the northeast. The Mexican Army was pursuing Houston and although, on March 20, he had the opportunity to strike back, he chose to wait for a better time. In April, the Mexican Army, under direct command of Santa Anna, approached Lynch's Ferry at the San Jacinto River. Santa Anna's army consisted of 1,200 to 1,300 soldiers and were surprised by Houston's force of 900 men who overwhelmed them on the afternoon of April 21. The Battle of San Jacinto lasted only 18 minutes amid vengeful cries "Remember the Alamo" and "Remember Goliad." In Houston's official report, it was listed that 630 Mexicans were killed and 730 were taken prisoner, compared to 9 Texans being killed. Santa Anna was captured while fleeing and was Madde to order his army to retreat to Mexico.

On May 14, while still a prisoner, Santa Anna signed the Treaties of Velasco… one was public and one was secret. The public treaty ended the war and recognized Texas. The secret treaty stated that Santa Anna was to return to Mexico and see to it that the Mexican Government adhered to the public treaty. While Santa

Anna was absent, the Mexican Government disposed of him and refused to recognize Texas. Mexico would continue to clash with Texas up to the Mexican American War.

Republic of Texas
Republica de Tejas (Spanish)
1836-1846

Motto: "Remember the Alamo" (1)

Capital:
San Antonio de Bexar (Mexican Texas)
San Felipe de Austin (1835, provisional)
Washington-on-the-Brazos (1836, interim)
Harrisburg (1836, interim)
Galveston (1836, interim)
Velasco (1836, interim)
Columbia (1836-1837)
Houston (1837-1839)
Austin (1839-1846)

Official language: English and Spanish

Other languages: German, French, Portuguese, Native languages (Caddo, Comanche)

Government: Unitary presidential constitutional republic

President
1836: David G. Burnet
1836-38: Sam Houston, 1st term

1838-41: Mirabeau B. Lamar
1841-44: Sam Houston, 2nd term
1844-46: Anson Jones

Vice President
1836: Lorenzo de Zavala
1836-38: Mirabeau B. Lamar
1838-41: David G. Burnet
1841-44: Edward Burleson
1844-45: Kenneth L. Anderson

Legislature: Congress
Upper House: Senate
Lower House: House of Representatives

Historical era: Western Expansion
Independence from Mexico: March 2, 1836
Annexation by the United States: December 29, 1845
Transfer of Power: February 19, 1846

William B. Travis
August 1, 1809 - March 6, 1836

Birth Name: William Barret Travis

Nickname(s): Buck [2]

Born: August 1, 1809
Saluda County, South Carolina

Died: March 6, 1836 (aged 26)
The Alamo - San Antonio, Texas

Allegiance: Republic of Texas

Service/branch: Texian Army

Years of service: 1835-1836

Rank: Lieutenant Colonel

Commands held: The Alamo

Battles/wars:
Texas Revolution (Siege of Bexar & Battle of the Alamo)

Chapter Six
William B. Travis
August 1, 1809 - March 6, 1836

William's parents were Mark and Jemima Travis, who lived in South Carolina. William's nickname as Buck. William had nine other siblings. When William was nine years old, his parents moved the family to Alabama where his Uncle Alexander lived. William grew up in the town of Sparta and received his education at the Sparta Academy, that his uncle established. He studied subjects such as Greek, Latin, history and mathematics. After a few years, Davis went to the Academy of Professor William H. McCurdy, in Claiborne, Alabama. After completing his education, at the age of 18, he got a position of an assistant teacher.

Wanting to get away from farm living, Travis moved to Claiborne permanently and began to study law. A famed lawyer, James Dellett, accepted Travis as an apprentice. Travis married Rosanna Cato, whom he met while he was an assistant teacher; they married on October 26, 1828. They had their first son, Charlie, a year later.

While still studying law, Travis was anxious to resume his career and join the high ranks of society. Travis started a newspaper called *The Claiborne Herald* which published stories ranging from congress, local notices, advertisements, adventures across the world's, etc., like most all newspapers do. Travis operated the newspaper himself and it made a modest income but not enough to support him and his family. The financial stress took a toll on *The Herald,* by accidentally making huge mistakes in the printing. He requested help at the newspaper but received none.

On February 27, 1829, Travis passed his law exam and received permission to have his own practice. He had borrowed $90 earlier to help with *The Harold*; now, he borrowed another $55.37 to open his law office. Now in debt with hardly any income, Travis took in three boarding students to help Rosanna with the work. Travis then purchased two slaves, however to maintain the slaves that put him further in debt. *The Herald* intended to be a weekly publication but the issues declined so that only six issues were published in the fall. By the end of the year, Travis still didn't have any help with *The Harold* thus it stopped being printed. With hardly any business with his law firm coming in, the debts kept mounting up; his earlier loans didn't get paid and more debts kept coming in. His law practice wasn't getting any attention. The clients trusted lawyers like Dellett more than they would Travis. At the end of his law practice, Travis received less than $4.00 and, by the spring of 1831, he was $834 in debt. Travis owed Dellett, along with others, filed suits for Travis' debt. Travis filed a plea for the case to be dismissed on the grounds that he was still considered a minor in parts of Alabama. Dellett forced Travis to stand in the courtroom yelling, "Gentleman, I make 'Proofest' of this infant!" Travis stood, humiliated, in a courtroom full of people laughing and the court's clerk issued orders to have him arrested on March 31, 1831.

During this time, Travis heard stories about Texas, which was an outlying state in the First Mexican Republic. In Texas, there were settlers coming in from the United States and Europe. There also was a big demand for lawyers to deal with the immigrants and land dealings so, he made a decision to go to Texas. Travis promised his wife, now pregnant with a second child, that he would be able to make enough money to pay back all the debts. Rosanna trusted him to return or send for her and the children. He did neither. Travis avoided arrest and left for Texas.

In 1831, upon his arrival in Mexican Texas, Travis purchased land from Stephen F. Austin. Austin appointed Travis as Counsel from the United States. Travis setup a law firm in Anahuac and helped setup a militia to oppose Mexican rule. Travis became a pivotal figure in the Anahuac Disturbance, which were conflicts that took place before the Texas Revolution and was the result of the tensions between the Mexican Government and the Texians Militia.

In 1832, a disturbance was triggered by a dispute about ownership of escaped slaves that a Mexican brigadier general, Juan Davis Bradburn, was keeping in a compound in Galveston. The slave owner hired Travis to try and get the slaves back; he was arrested twice by Bradburn, including the act of sending a threatening letter to Bradburn. Bradburn, himself, was convinced that Austin was part of the revolt against the Mexican Government's rule.

The Anglo Texian militia came to free Travis; he encouraged them to attack the Mexicans during the negotiation. Bradburn threatened to shoot Travis if they did. While Austin was freed during the negotiations, there was a conflict that led to six deaths and the Turtle Bayou Resolutions.

A second dispute happened on June 17, 1835, following the tensions of the Anti-Tax Protest by Texians and the organization of the group called "The Citizens of Texas." Briscoe and Harris were two men who organized a stunt to test the tax laws and were arrested by a Mexican commander, Captain Antonio Tenorio. A Texian, William Smith, was shot by soldiers who were escorting Briscoe and Harris. Travis gathered a Texian militia, authorized by Political Chief Peter Miller, when the news of the arrest was heard. Travis commandeered a vessel and sailed to Anahuac. His 25 man force quickly got 40 Mexican troops to surrender. Travis freed the Texians and expelled the Mexican troops. Because Travis acted without community support, he apologized to avoid endangering Stephen F. Austin, who was in Mexico City at the time. Mexican military demanded the surrender of Travis for trial but the colonists opposed it. Travis was commissioned as a Lieutenant Colonel of the Calvary and became the Chief Recruiting Officer for the new Texian Army. Travis was ordered to raise a company of soldiers to reinforce the Texians at the Alamo, by Governor Henry Smith. At the time, the Alamo was commanded by James C. Nell.

Travis died on March 6, 1836, following a 13 day siege by Santa Anna's Mexican Army.

<u>James Bowie</u>
1796 - March 6, 1836

Nickname(s): Jim Bowie, Santiago Bowie

Born: c. 1796
Logan County, Kentucky, U.S.

Died: March 6, 1836 (aged 26)
Alamo Mission - San Antonio, Texas

Allegiance: Republic of Texas

Years of service: 1835-1836

Rank: Colonel

Unit: Texian volunteer army

Commands held: The Alamo, San Antonio

Battles/wars:
- Texas Revolution
- Long Expedition
- Battle of Nacogdoches
- Battle of Concepcion
- Grass Fight
- Battle of the Alamo

Chapter Seven
James Bowie
1796 - March 6, 1836

Bowie was an American pioneer, slave smuggler, trader and soldier. Bowie was born in Kentucky but raised in Louisiana. He worked as a land speculator but gained his fame starting during a sandbar fight, in 1827. What started as a duel between two men, ended up with Bowie being shot and stabbed; he killed the Sheriff of Rapids Parish with his large knife. This and other stories of Bowie's adventures led to the popularity of the Bowie knife.

Bowie moved to Texas, in 1830, and became a Mexican citizen. He married the Vice Governor of the Province's daughter; Juan Martin de Veramendi's daughter's name was Ursula de Veramendi. Bowie led an expedition to find the lost San Saba Mine. His small party was attacked by a large Native American raiding party. He enhanced his reputation but he never located the mine. During the outbreak of the Texas Revolution, Bowie joined the militia. He led forces in the Battle of Concepcion and the Grass Fight. Bowie arrived at the Alamo, in January 1836. He commanded the volunteer forces until his illness caused him to be bedridden. He died, on March 6, along with other Alamo defenders.

Early Years

Bowie's parents were Reason and Elve Bowie. His father was wounded in the American Revolutionary War and, in 1282, married Elve, who was the one that nursed him back to health.

The Bowies first settled in Georgia, then moved to Kentucky. His father owned slaves, cattle and horses. The next year, they acquired 200 acres along the Red River. In 1800, they sold that property and moved to what is now Missouri. In 1802, they moved to Spanish Louisiana and settled in Bushley Bayou in what soon became Rapides Parish. In 1804, the family moved again to Bayou Teche, in Louisiana, and then found a permanent home in Opelousas, in 1812. Bowie was the ninth out of ten children that grew up on the frontier working at a young age clearing, planting and harvesting. All the children learned to read and write in English, but James and his elder brother, Rezin, could also read and write in Spanish and French. All the children were proficient and learned how to survive on the frontier, but James had a reputation as being fearless thus he became proficient with rifles, pistols and knives.

James and Rezin enlisted, in response for volunteers by General Andrew Jackson, during the War of 1812. After mustering out of the militia, Bowie settled in Rapides Parish and worked at sawing planks and lumber; he floated them down the bayou for sale. In 1819, he joined the long expedition to help liberate Texas from Spanish rule. They captured Nacogdoches and declared Texas as an Independent Republic. He went back to Louisiana before the invasion was repelled by the Spanish troops.

Land Speculator and Slave Smuggler

In 1820, both James and Resin were given ten slaves, horses and cattle by their father before he died. Together, they developed several large estates in LaFourch Parish and Opelousas. The brothers were hoping land prices would be good because Louisiana's population was growing. Not having the money to purchase large tracts of land, they entered a partnership with a pirate, Jean Lafitte. At that time, the United States outlawed importation of slaves. Most of the southern states offered about half of what slaves would earn at an auction for informing of illegal slave trading.

Bowie made trips to Lafitte's compound on Galveston Island and brought back slaves to the customs house and informed them on his own actions. When the Customs Office auctioned off the slaves, Bowie would buy them and still receive back half the price he had paid - that was allowed by the state's law. He could take the slaves to New Orleans or further up the Mississippi and sell them for greater market value. By using this scheme, the brothers collected $65,000.00 to use on their land speculation. In 1825, the two brothers, along with their younger brother Stephen, purchased Acadia Plantation near Thibodaux. There, within two years, they built the first steam mill in Louisiana for grinding sugarcane. On February 12, 1831, they sold it and 65 slaves for $90,000.00 and, with the profits, they purchased a plantation in Arkansas.

Bowie and his brother John were involved in a major Arkansas court case, over land speculation, in the late 1820s. In 1803, the United States purchased the Louisiana Territory. At that time, it promised to honor all former land grant claims made to French and Spanish colonists. Efforts were made for 20 years to establish who owned what land. In May 1824, Congress authorized the Superior Court of each territory to hear suits on those who claim they had been overlooked.

In late 1827, the Arkansas Superior Court had received 126 claims from residents claiming to have purchased land in former Spanish grants from the Bowie brothers. It was originally confirmed that the claims and decisions were reversed, in February 1831. With further research, it showed the land had never belonged to the Bowies and the original land grant had been forged. When the disgruntled purchasers decided to sue the Bowies, they discovered the documents had been removed from the court; without evidence, they declined to sue.

Bowie Knife

Bowie became internationally famous over a duel with Norris Wright who was Sheriff of Rapides. Bowie supported Wright's opponent and Wright, being a banker, turned down a loan to Bowie. Wright fired a shot at Bowie during a confrontation which, after, Bowie resolved to carry his hunting knife at all times; the knife's blade was 9.25 inches long and 1.5 inches wide. Bowie and Wright attended a duel on a sandbar near Natchez, Mississippi. Bowie supported Samuel Levi Wells III while Wright supported the opponent, Dr. Thomas Harris Maddox. The two fired their weapons and missed each other and settled their duel with a handshake. There were others in the group that felt a dislike for each other and began to fight. Bowie was shot in the hip and, as he was getting back on his feet, he drew his knife and charged his attacker. The man hit Bowie over the head with his pistol, knocking him to the ground. While on the ground, Wright shot at him and missed. Bowie returned fire, possibly hitting Wright. Wright drew his sword and stabbed Bowie; as he went to place his foot on Bowie's chest to retrieve his sword, Bowie pulled him down and gutted him with his knife. Wright died instantly and Bowie, with Wright's sword still protruding from his chest, was shot and stabbed again by another member of the group. Doctors that were at the duel removed the bullets from Bowie and bandaged his other wounds.

Newspapers picked up this story and named it "*Sandbar Fight*." It was noted that Bowie had an unusual knife and he gained the reputation of a superb knife fighter, which was set across the south. Some say Bowie designed his knife; some say a knife maker in Arkansas made it, but his brother, Rezin, said he designed it. Rezin's grandchildren said Rezin only supervised his blacksmith, who was the designer of the knife. In subsequent battles, which Bowie was in, he used his knife in self-defense.

The Bowie knife became so popular, many craftsmen and manufacturers made their own versions. Major cities in the old southwest had "Bowie Knife Schools" that taught the art of cut, thrust and parry. By the early 1830s, in Great Britain, the Bowie knife and Bowie's fame was reached. British manufacturers were producing and shipping knives to the United States.

A Bowie knife is generally considered to have a blade 8.25 inches long and 1.25 inches wide, a curved point and a sharp edge on both sides. It also has a cross guard to protect the user's hand.

Established in Texas, in 1828, Bowie recovered from his wounds from the sandbar fight. He decided to move to Coahuila, Texas, which at that time was a state in the Mexican Federation. In 1824, Mexico banned all religions except for Roman Catholicism, in which Bowie was baptized in. For the next 18 months, Bowie traveled around Louisiana and Mississippi.

In 1829, Bowie became engaged to Cecilia Wells, who died two weeks before they were married. Bowie left Louisiana on January 1, 1830, to live in Texas permanently. Bowie proceeded to San Antonio de Bexar that had a population of 2,500, of mostly Mexican decent. Later that year, Bowie was elected Commander of the Texas Rangers with the rank of Colonel. The Rangers were not officially organized until 1835. Austin had founded the Rangers by hiring 30 men to protect the colonists.

Bowie renounced his American citizenship and became a Mexican citizen, on September 30, 1830. He promised to build textile mills in the state of Coahuila, Texas. He then entered a partnership with Veramendi to build cotton and wool mills in Saltillo. By being a citizen, Bowie was allowed to buy up to 11 leagues of public land. He then convinced 14 or 15 other citizens to apply for land and transfer it to him; by doing this, it established him with 700,000 acres for speculation. Bowie may have been the first to get settlers to apply for grants which could be sold in bulk to speculators, as Bowie had. In 1834 and 1835, the Mexican Government passed laws that stopped most land speculation.

Bowie married the daughter of his business partner, 19 year old Maria Ursula de Veramendi, on April 25,

1831. He had to sign a dowry contract promising to pay his bride 15,000 pesos, approximately $15,000 at the time, in cash or property. He had two years to pay her in. Bowie claimed, at the time, had had $223,000, mostly in land of questionable title. Bowie also lied, stating he was 30 years old rather than 35.

Bowie and his wife built a house in San Antonio, on land her father had given them near the San Jose Mission. Shortly after, they moved into the Veramendi Palace to live with Ursula's parents; Ursula's parents also provided them with spending money. The couple had two children, Marie Elve, on March 20, 1832 and James Veramendi Bowie, on July 18, 1833.

Maria Ursula, her parents and both children died, in September 1833, during a Cholera epidemic that swept through the south.

Los Almagres Mine

Right after his marriage, Bowie became interested and fascinated in the story of the "Los Almagres Mine." The mine was also known as the "Lost San Saba Mine." According to legend, the mine was operated by Native Americans before being seized by the Spanish.

Bowie obtained permission from the Mexican Government to lead an expedition into Indian Territory to search for the silver mine. Bowie, his brother Rezin and 10 others set out for San Saba to search for the mine, on November 2, 1831. It was reported that within six miles of their destination, they came across a raiding party of 120 Tawakoni and Waco, plus 40 Caddo. Their attempt to parley failed, Bowie and his group fought for their lives for 13 hours.

It was reported that Bowie lost one man and the Indians lost more than 40 men with 30 wounded. A party of friendly Comanche rode into San Antonio with word that the raiding party outnumbered Bowie's party by 14 to 1. The people of San Antonio believed that Bowie's expedition must have perished; to the town's surprise, Bowie's expedition returned home. The next month, he set out again with a larger expedition but returned home, again, after 2.5 months, empty handed. Bowie never talked about his exploits, despite his increasing fame. Captain William Y. Lacey, who spent eight months in the wilderness with him, said, "He was a humble man who never used profanity or vulgarities."

In July 1832, Bowie joined a group of Texans and marched to Nacogdoches to "present their demands" to Piedras about the way the Mexican Government was treating the colonists. They were attacked by a force of 100 Mexican calvary. The Texans returned fire and the "Battle of Nacogdoches" began.

Bowie later served as a delegate, to the Convention of 1833, that formally requested Texas become its own state within the Mexican Federation.

Later on, a Cholera epidemic struck Texas. Bowie, to prevent the epidemic, sent his family to the family estate, in Monclova, with his brother-in-law and his wife's parents. In September, his wife, children, his wife's brother and parents died of the disease. Bowie, on business, did not find out until November. After that, he began drinking and being careless.

The following year Bowie was back into land speculation when the Mexican Government passed new laws allowing the sale of land in Texas. He was appointed commissioner and had the task of promoting settlement in the area. In May of 1835, his appointment ended when President Antonio Lopez de Santa Anna abolished the Texas Government and ordered that all Texans, including Bowie, be arrested for doing business in Monclova. The Texians wanted war with Santa Anna and Bowie worked with William B. Travis, who was leader of the War Department, to gain his support. During the Battle of Gonzalez, which was the start of the Texas Revolution. October 2, 1835, Stephen F. Austin formed an army of 500 men to march on San Antonio. Fannin and Bowie, who was now a colonel in the Volunteer Militia, were sent to scout around the missions for supplies for the army. The scouting party left with 92 men and discovered a good defensive position near Mission Conception; at that time, they requested Austin's army to join them. On the morning of October 28, Mexican General Domingo Ugartechea led a force of 300 infantry and calvary soldiers against the Texian forces… The Battle of Conception.

The Battle of Conception

An hour after the battle ended, Austin arrived with the rest of the army to begin the siege of San Antonio de Bexar.

On November 3, 1835, Texas declared itself as an independent state. At some point, Bowie appeared before the council asking for a commission but his request was refused. Houston offered Bowie a commission as an officer on his staff but Bowie refused because he wanted to be in the midst of the fighting. He then enlisted in the Army under Fannin as a private. He distinguished himself in the "Grass Fight" on November 26.

Battle of the Alamo

Bowie perished with the rest of the defenders on March 6, 1836. Bowie's body was ordered to be buried because he was too brave of a man to be burned.

<u>Davy Crockett</u>
August 17, 1786 - March 6, 1836

**Member of the
U.S. House Of Representatives
From Tennessee**

In office: March 4, 1827 - March 4, 1831

Preceded by: Adam Rankin Alexander

Succeeded by: William Fitzgerald

Constituency: 9th district

In office: March 4, 1833 - March 4, 1835

Preceded by: *District created*

Succeeded by: Adam Huntsman

Constituency: 12th district

Personal details
Born: David Crockett
August 17, 1786
Limestone, Greene County, Tennessee
(at the time, part of North Carolina), U.S.

Died: March 6, 1836 (aged 49)
Alamo Mission, San Antonio, Texas, U.S.

Chapter Eight
Davy Crockett
August 17, 1786 - March 6, 1836

John Crockett was born in 1753, in Frederick County, Virginia. In 1768, the family moved to Tryon County, North Carolina. In 1776, they moved again to Hawkins County - known now as Tennessee.

John married Rebecca Hawkins, in 1780, and had a son, David, born on August 17, 1786. David was born in what is now known as Greene County, Tennessee - at the time, it was a part of North Carolina, near the community of Limestone.

John was having trouble making ends meet and moved the family to Lick Creek, in 1792. John sold that land and moved the family again, in 1794. There, him and his partner built a gristmill and the Crockett homestead. A flood destroyed the gristmill and the homestead and, again, the Crocketts moved to Mossy Creek, in Jefferson County, Tennessee. In 1795, John lost his property in bankruptcy. The family moved again onto a property owned by a Quaker named John Canady. John built a tavern on a stage coach line in the Southwest Territory.

When David turned 12 years old, he hired out and worked on cattle drives to help get his father out of debt. One of his drives was a 400 mile trip to Virginia. When the debts were paid off, his father told him he was free to leave. David went back to his employer, John Canady, where he stayed for four years.

Marriage

David fell in love with his employer's niece, who was already engaged to John Canady's son, Robert. While being part of the wedding party, Crockett met Margaret Elder and persuaded her to marry him. The marriage contract was drawn up, on October 21, 1805, but Margaret had become engaged to another man at the same time and married him instead of Crockett. He met Polly Finley and her mother, Jean, at a harvest festival.

Jean Finley was friendly to Crockett but she didn't feel that he was right for her daughter. He showed his intentions to marry Polly, whether the marriage was allowed to take place in her parent's home or not. David arranged for the Justice of the Peace and got the marriage license on August 12, 1806. He rode to Polly's house, on August 16, with his family and friends.

Being determined to ride off and marry Polly somewhere else, Polly's father pleaded that they get married at home. Crockett agreed after Jean apologized for her past treatment of him. David and Polly settled down on a piece of land near her parent's home.

Their first child, John Wesley Crockett, later became a United States Congressman. He was born on July 10, 1807. They had their second child, William Finley Crockett, on November 23, 1808. The family then moved to Lincoln County. They had a third child, Margaret Finley Crockett, born on November 25, 1812. In 1813, the Crocketts moved to Franklin County. Crockett's wife died in March 1815. That same year, he married the widow Elizabeth Patton, who had a daughter and son - Margaret and George. David and Elizabeth had a son, Robert Patton, who was born on September 16, 1816. They had a daughter, Rebecca Elvira, born on December 25, 1818. They also had a daughter, Matilda, born on August 2, 1821.

Tennessee Milita Service

The Fort Mims Massacre was on August 30, 1813. It happened near Mobile, Mississippi Territory. Crockett enlisted as a scout on September 30. He was to serve for an initial term of 90 days under Colonel John Coffee in the Francis Jones Company of Mounted Riflemen.

They marched south to current day Alabama and took part in active fighting. Crockett hunted wild game to feed the soldiers and that suited him better than killing the Creek warriors during the Creek War.

The War of 1812 was being waged at the same time as the Creek War. After the Treat of Fort Jackson was signed, in August 1814, Andrew Jackson, of the U.S. Army, wanted the British forces ousted out of Spanish Florida. He requested the help from the Tennessee Militia. Crockett re-enlisted for a 6 month term as a third sergeant in the Tennessee Mounted Gunman, under Captain John Cowan, on September 28, 1814. Crockett's unit saw little action because they were days behind the rest of the troops. They spent most of the time focusing on foraging for food. In December, Crockett returned home still being on military reserve status until March 1815. He hired a young man to fulfill the remainder of his service.

Public Career

Crockett moved his family to a new location in Lawrence County. This is where he first entered public office. He was made commissioner and helped configure the new county boundaries. He was appointed the County Justice of the Peace, on November 25. On March 27, 1818, he defeated Daniel Matthews and was elected Lieutenant Colonel of the Fifty-Seventh Regiment of the Tennessee Militia. By 1819, he was operating multiple businesses and felt his public responsibilities were taking too much time from his family and businesses so, he resigned the office of the Justice of the Peace and his position with the regiment.

Tennessee General Assembly

In 1821, Crockett resigned his commissioner position and successfully ran for a seat in the Tennessee General Assembly representing Lawrence and Hickman Counties. In 1821, he was appointed to the Propositions and Grievances Committee.

He spent his entire legislative career fighting for the impoverished settler's rights, who felt they would lose the title of their land due to the state's complicated system of grants.

Less than 2 weeks after Crockett's election, the Tennessee River flooded and destroyed Crockett's businesses. Elizabeth's father, Robert Patton, deeded 800 acres of his Carroll County land to Crockett. Crockett sold off most of the property to pay off his debts and moved his family on the Remainy Property near the Obion River, that remained in Carroll County until 1825; the boundaries were reconfigured and it was put into Gibson.

In 1823, Crockett won the seat in General Assembly representing the counties of Carroll, Humphreys, Perry, Henderson and Madison. He served the first session, September through November 1823 and the second session, September through November 1824. He was championing the impoverished farmer's rights.

United States House of Representatives

On October 25, 1824, Crockett notified his intentions of running for a seat in the House of Representatives, in the election of 1825. He lost that election to incumbent, Adam Rankin Alexander. In 1826, a meeting with Memphis Mayor Marcus Brutus Winchester gave him encouragement to try again, to win a seat in Congress. On September 15, 1826, the Jackson Gazette published a letter from Crockett announcing his intentions of challenging Rankin again and stating his opposition to the policies of President John Quincy Adams, Secretary of State Henry Clay and to Rankin's position on the cotton tariffs. A militia veteran, William Arnold, also entered the race, although Crockett defeated both his political opponents for the 1827-1829 term.

Jackson was elected president, in 1828. Crockett focused on the setters getting a fair deal, offering H.R. 27 Amendment to a bill sponsored by James K. Polk. Crockett defeated Ranking once again and won the election, on October 25, 1824. He introduced H.R. 185 Amendment to the Land Bill, on January 29, 1830.

On February 25, 1830, he introduced a resolution to the abolish the United States Military Academy at West Point because he felt the public money was to benefit the sons of the wealthy men.

Crockett was against Congress for giving $100,000 to the widow of Stephen Decatur, stating that Congress didn't have the power to do that. He was opposed to Jackson's 1830 Indian Removal Act and was the only one to vote against it from the Tennessee Delegation. He received a letter, on January 13, 1831, from Cherokee Chief John Ross, thanking him for his vote. His vote was not popular with his own district and he was defeated, in 1831, by William Fitzgerald.

Crockett ran again, in 1833, and defeated Fitzgerald; he returned to Congress until 1835. He was defeated in reelection, in August 1835, by Adam Huntsman. During his last term, he worked with Kentucky Congressman Thomas Chilton to write his autobiography and published it, in 1834, as *A Narrative of the Life of David Crockett*, written by himself. "I told the people of my district that I would serve them as faithfully as I had done, but if not, they might go to hell, and I would go to Texas."

Texas Revolution

On November 1, 1835, he left his home in Rutherford, in West Tennessee, with 3 other men to explore Texas. His youngest child, Matilda, wrote that she distinctly remembered the last time she saw her father.

> *"He was dressed in his hunting suit, wearing a coonskin cap, and carried a fine rifle presented*

to him by friends in Philadelphia. He seemed very confident the morning he went away that he would soon have us all join him in Texas."

Crockett and 30 well armed men traveled to Jackson, Tennessee, where he gave a speech on the steps of the Madison County Courthouse. On November 12, 1835, they arrived in Little Rock, Arkansas. The local newspapers and hundreds of people swarmed into town to get a look at Crockett. A group of leading citizens put on a dinner at the Jeffries Hotel in his honor. Crockett spoke mainly about Texas independence and Washington politics.

In January 1836, Crockett arrived in Nocogdoches, Texas. On January 14, he and 65 men signed an oath before Judge John Forbes to the Provisional Government of Texas for 6 months. For volunteering, each man was promised 4,600 acres of land as payment. Crockett and 5 other men left, on February 6, to San Antonio de Bexar and camped just outside of town. Crockett and his men arrived at the Alamo Mission, in San Antonio, on February 8, 1836. On February 23, General Antonio Lopez de Santa Anna initiated a siege on the Mission. The siege ended, on March 6, when the Mexican soldiers attacked just before dawn while the defenders were sleeping. The Battle of the Alamo lasted 90 minutes and all the defenders were killed.

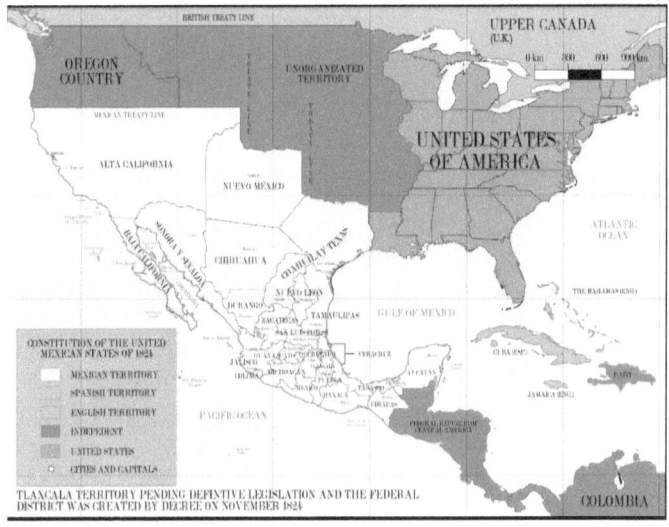

First Federal Republic of Mexico in 1824. Coahuila y Tejas is the northeasternmost state.

Before the Battle of the Alamo in 1836

<u>Sam Houston</u>
March 2, 1793 - July 26, 1863

Personal Details

Born: Samuel Houston
March 2, 1793 - Rockbridge, Virginia, U.S.

Died: July 26, 1863 (aged 70)
Huntsville, Texas, C.S.

Political Party: Democratic-Republican (before 1830)
Democratic (1846-1854)
Know Nothing (1855-1856)
Independent (1856-1863)

Spouse(s):
Eliza Allen (m. 1829; div. 1837)
Tiana Rogers (m. 1830; annulled 1832)
Margaret Lea (m. 1840)

Education: Maryville College

Military Service

Allegiance: United States, Republic of Texas

Branch/service: United States Army, Texan Army

Years of Service: 1813-1818 (U.S. Army)
1835-1836 (Texas Army)
Rank: First Lieutenant (U.S. Army)
Major General (Texan Army)

Unit: 39th Infantry Regiment (U.S. Army)

Commands: Army of the Republic of Texas (Texan Army)

Battles/Wars

War of 1812
Creek War - Battle of Horseshoe Bend
Texas Revolution - Battle of San Jacinto

7th Governor of Texas

In office: December 21, 1859 - March 15, 1861
Lieutenant: Edward Clark
Preceded by: Hardin Richard Runnels
Succeeded by: Edward Clark

United States Senator from Texas

In office: February 21, 1846 - March 3, 1859
Preceded by: Seat established
Succeeded by: John Hemphill

1st and 3rd President of Texas

In office: December 21, 1841 - December 9, 1844
Vice President: Edward Burleson
Preceded by: Mirabeau B. Lamar
Succeeded by: Anson Jones

In office: October 22, 1836 - December 10, 1838
Vice President: Mirabeau B. Lamar
Preceded by: David G. Burnet (acting)
Succeeded by: Mirabeau B. Lamar

Member of the Texas House of Representatives From the San Augustine District

In office: 1839 - 1841

6th Governor of Tennessee

In office: October 1, 1827 - April 16, 1829
Lieutenant: William Hall
Preceded by: William Carroll
Succeeded by: William Hall

Member of the U.S. House of Representatives From Tennessee's 7th District

In office: March 4, 1823 - March 3, 1827
Preceded by: Constituency established
Succeeded by: John Bell

Chapter Nine
Sam Houston
March 2, 1793 - July 26, 1863

March 2, 1793 - July 26, 1863, Houston was a general and a statesman who played a big role in the Texas Revolution.

He was born in Rockbridge County, Virginia. When Houston was a teenager his family migrated to Maryville, Tennessee. Houston lived with the Cherokee Indians for about three years after he ran away from home. When he lived there, he was known as the Raven. During the War of 1812, he serviced under General Andrew Jackson. In 1823, Houston won the election to the United States House of Representatives.

He strongly supported Jackson's presidential candidacies and, in 1827, was elected as Governor of Tennessee. In 1829, Houston divorced his first wife, resigned from office and moved to Arkansas Territory.

In 1832, Houston moved and settled in Texas. He helped organize Texas' Government after the Battle of Gonzalez.

He was selected as the top ranking official in the Texian Army and led the army to victory during the Battle of San Jacinto - the decisive battle in Texas' war of independence against Mexico.

Houston won the election of 1836 as president and

left off, in 1838, due to term limits. He ran again, in 1842, and won the presidential election again. In 1845, Houston played a big role in the annexation of Texas to the United States.

In 1846, he was elected to represent Texas in the United States Senate. He joined the Democratic Party and supported President James K. Polk's prosecution of the Mexican-American War. He voted for the Compromise of 1850, which settled many territorial issues over the Mexican-American War and the annexation of Texas. He later voted against the Kansas-Nebraska Act because he believed it would increase the tension over slavery and this led him to leave the Democratic Party. He was unsuccessful as a candidate for presidential nomination in 1856 and in 1860. In 1859, Houston won the election for Governor of Texas. He opposed the succession and unsuccessfully sought to keep Texas out of the Confederate States of America. He was forced out of office in 1861 and died in 1863. Houston's name has been honored in many ways.

Houston's Early Life

Samuel Houston was born in Rockbridge County, Virginia, on March 2, 1793, to Samuel Houston and Elizabeth Payton. Houston's parents settled in Colonial America and were of Scottish and Irish descents.

Houston had five brothers and three sisters. His father passed away as he was planning to sell Timber Ridge and move to Tennessee. His mother, Elizabeth, followed through because the land was less expensive there. Elizabeth cleared the land and built their house in Maryville, of Blount County, Tennessee. Three of her oldest children passed away within a few years after they arrived. Same was had the type of disposition that like to explore the frontier. Sam wasn't interested in farming or running the store so, at the age of 16, he left home to live with the Cherokee Indian Tribe. Houston learned the Cherokee language and was give the name of Raven.

The War of 1812

Houston enlisted into the United States Army in 1812. At the time, they were engaged in a war against Britain and Britain's Native American allies. Houston quickly rose to the rank of third lieutenant.

By 1814, his 39th Regiment became in charge by General Andrew Jackson who was in charge of putting an end to the raids. Houston was badly wounded in the Battle of Horseshoe Bend during the Creek War. The Army doctors expected Houston would not live from his wounds... he survived. Houston was promoted to second lieutenant and, in early 1817, he was assigned a clerical position, in Nashville, serving under the adjutant general. Later that year, General Jackson appointed Houston to handle the removal of the Cherokee from East Tennessee. In February 1818, he wore Native American dress to a meeting between Secretary of War John C. Calhoun and the Cherokee leaders... for this, he received a strong reprimand. Angry over the incident with Calhoun and an investigation of his activities, Houston resigned from the Army in 1818. He helped the Cherokee resettle in the Arkansas Territory and continued to act as a government liaison with the Cherokee.

Houston's Early Political Career

Houston began an apprenticeship under Judge James Trimble, in Nashville, after he left government service. He soon won his state bar and opened his practice. He won the election as District Attorney for Nashville, in 1819. Houston strongly supported Andrew Jackson's candidacy in the 1824 presidential election.

Jackson lost the election to John Quincy Adams. Houston won the election for Governor of Tennessee with the backing of Andrew Jackson, in 1827. Governor Houston made improvements, such as canals and lowering prices of land for homesteaders.

He aided Andrew Jackson's successful campaign for the 1828 presidential election.

Houston married Eliza Allen, in January 1829. The marriage didn't last and finally collapsed. Shortly after his marriage collapsed, Houston resigned as Governor of Tennessee. He left office and went back to Arkansas to rejoin the Cherokee.

Political Exile

With Houston's experience with the government, the Cherokee and local Native American tribes asked Houston to mediate disputes and communicate their needs to the Jackson administration. Anticipating the removal of the rest of Cherokee establishments of the Mississippi River, Houston made a bid to supply rations for their journey but it was unsuccessful. In

1832, Congressman William Stanbery accused Houston of placing a fraudulent bid, in 1830, regarding the incident. Houston beat Stanbery with a cane. The House of Representatives brought Houston to trial. By a vote of 106 to 89, Houston was convicted and the federal court also required Houston to pay $500.00 in damages.

Texas Revolution

In mid-1832, Houston was convinced by two of his friends, William H. Wharton and John A. Wharton, to come to the Mexican Possession of Texas. At this time, Texas was part of the Coahuila y Tejas. The settlers and the Whartons did not like living under the Mexican rules. Houston arrived into Texas, in December of 1832. Shortly after, he was granted land and elected to represent Nacogdoches, Texas, at the Convention of 1833, to draw up a petition to Mexico for statehood. A committee was chosen to draw up a state constitution.

Stephen F. Austin partitioned the Mexican Government for statehood but was unable to meet an agreement. In 1834, Antonio Lopez de Santa Anna took over presidency and had Austin arrested. The Texas Revolution broke out, in 1834, with the Battle of Gonzales between the Texas forces and the Mexican Army.

Houston, Austin and others organized the Consultation into a provisional government for Texas.

Shortly after, the delegates, along with Houston, voted for a measure that demanded for Texas statehood. Houston was appointed a Major General in the Texas Army as the highest ranking officer by the

Consultation. He was appointed as the Commander and Chief of the Texas Army but had no control over the militia units of the Texian Army.

When the convention received the plea for help from William B. Travis at the Alamo, who was the commander of the Texian forces, who was under siege by Santa Anna. Houston was confirmed to command the Texian forces but the Alamo was lost before he could organize his forces at Gonzales. Learning that Santa Anna had killed all the defenders at the Alamo outraged the Texians and Houston lost men from desertion.

With any 350 men against Santa Anna, Houston retreated east across the Colorado River. Even through the government and his subordinates continued to urge him to attack, he kept moving east. Houston kept telling his soldiers that we are only a few and the only army in Texas. If we are beaten, the fate of Texas is sealed.

In mid-April 1836, Santa Anna had split up his forces and caught up to Houston. Santa Anna's forces were 1,350 soldiers compared to Houston's 783 men who were trapped in the marsh. Instead of Santa Anna attacking, he ordered his men to make camp. On April 21, Houston ordered the attack on the Mexican Army which is known as "The Battle of San Jacinto."

During the battle, Houston's horse was shot from under him and his ankle was shattered by a bullet. A detachment of Texians captured Santa Anna and he was forced to sign the Treaty of Velasco, granting Texas independence. Houston stayed for negotiations and then was taken to the United States for treatment of his ankle.

President of Texas

With the victory of San Jacinto that made Houston hero, he was elected president, in 1836, defeating Stephen F. Austin.

On October 22, 1836, Houston took office after Interim President David G. Burnet resigned. As Houston was challenged to make a new government, the voters were expressing their desires of being annexed by the United States. Trying to normalize relations with Mexico, Houston released Santa Anna, even though he was getting resistance from the legislature.

U.S. President Andrew Jackson, concerned about upsetting the balance between free states and slave states, refused to push for annexation of Texas. He did grant Texas diplomatic recognition. In 1837, the government moved the capital to the city of Houston, named after the county's new president, Sam Houston.

The Texas Constitution barred presidents to seek a second term; Houston left office in, 1838. Mirabeau B. Lamar succeeded Houston as President of Texas. The Lamar administration launched a war against the Cherokee and also removed many of Houston's appointees from office. Lamar also moved the capital to Austin, Texas. Houston open a legal practice and co-founded a land company. In 1839, Houston was elected to the Texas House of Representatives, representing San Augustine County.

The Texas presidential election, of 1841, was won by Houston, defeating Burnet. At that time, the Republic was in a difficult financial situation. Lamar had stirred up tension, with Mexico, with the Santa Fe

Expedition along with rumors and fears that Santa Anna would invade Texas. Houston hoped that the influence of the French and British would encourage the United States to annex Texas.

In 1844, Texas and the United States signed an Annexation Treaty. There wasn't enough support in Congress and the United States Senate rejected the annexation. Henry Clay and Martin Van Buren both opposed the annexation of Texas. By opposing the annexation, it hurt Van Buren's candidacy and he was defeated by James K. Polk, who was an old friend of Houston's. At the Democratic National Convention of 1844, Polk defeated Clay in the general election, giving the backers of the annexation an electoral mandate. Houston's term ended, in December 1844, and was succeeded by Anton Jones. Tyler used Polk's victory to convince Congress to approve the annexation of Texas.

Texas officially became the 28th state on December 29, 1845.

Mexican-American War and Aftermath
1846-1853

In February 1846, Houston and Rusk were elected by the Texas Legislature as Texas' two inaugural U.S. Senators.

Houston is the only former foreign head of state to have served in U.S. Congress. He was the first to serve as governor of a state and to be elected to the U.S. Senate by another state. In 1846, Houston wanted the annexation of Oregon. Later, in 1846, the United States and Britain reached an agreement to split Oregon under the "Oregon Treaty." During that time, General Zachary Taylor was ordered by Polk to lead the U.S. Army to the Rio Grande, which was set as the border by the Treaty of Velasco; Mexico claimed that the Nueces River was the border.

With the skirmish between Taylor's army and the Mexican Army, the Mexican-American War broke out, in April 1846. The United States defeated Mexico after two years of fighting. The "Treaty of Guadalupe Hidalgo" acquired the cession.

Mexico also recognized the Rio Grande as the true border between Mexico and the United States. After the war, disputes over the extensions of slavery into territories raised tension and Houston voted for the Oregon Bill of 1848, organizing Oregon as a free territory.

Houston said he would be the last man to do anything injurious to the south, but he did not think that on occasions that we are justified in agitating slavery. He supported the Compromise of 1850; under the Compromise, California became a free state, the slave trade was prohibited in the District of Columbia, a more stringent slave law was passed, and the Utah Territory and New Mexico Territory were established. Texas gave up some of New Mexico but kept El Paso, Texas. Houston tried to get the Democratic nomination, in the 1852 presidential election, but the Convention nominated Franklin Pierce, who won the election.

Pierce and Buchanan Administration
1853-1859

The Kansas-Nebraska Act of 1854 was led by Senator A. Douglas, which organized the territories of Kansas and

Nebraska. This act repealed the Missouri Compromise that had banned slavery in territories north of parallel 36° 30' north. Houston voted against the Act because he believed the Native Americans would lose much of their land and, also, that it would bring more tension over slavery. Houston's opposing led to his departure of the Democratic Party. In 1855, Houston began to associate with the American Party, a political wing of the Unionist Know Nothing Movement - the growing influence of Catholic voters - though he was against barring Catholics from holding office. He like the Know Nothings support of the Native American's state.

Houston was after the presidential nomination at the Know Nothings Party's 1856 National Convention, but they nominated former President Millar Fillmore.

Houston decided to support Fillmore, but despite his support, the American Party split over slavery. The 1856 presidential election was won by Democrat James Buchanan. Houston announced his candidacy for governor but Runnels defeated him. It was the only electoral defeat in his career. The Texas Legislature denied him re-election in the Senate. Houston rejected call for him to resign and served the end of his term in 1859.

Governor of Texas

In 1859, Houston defeated Runnels during the election because of Runnel's unpopularity over state issues. Houston and John Bell were the only two contenders for the presidential nomination for the new Constitutional Unionist Party. Bell clinched the nomination but, nonetheless, some of Houston's Texas supporters nominate him for president, in April 1860.

In August 1860, Houston announced that he would not be a candidate for president. Houston campaigned across Texas, calling all Texans to rest those who advocated for secession if Republican Abraham Lincoln was to win the 1860 election.

Lincoln did win the 1860 presidential election and several of the southern states seceded from the United States and formed the Confederate States of America. A Texas political convention voted to secede from the United States, on February 1, 1861.

Houston said Texas was once again an independent republic and refused to recognize the Authority of Texas joining the Confederacy. Houston refused to swear to the Oath of Confederacy so the legislature declared the governorship vacant but he did not recognize the validity of his removal. He did not attempt to remain in office. His successor, Edward Clark, was sworn in, on March 18.

Retirement and Death

Houston returned to his home in Galveston but later moved to Huntsville, Texas. Houston was shunned by many Texas leaders but he kept in contact with Ashbel Smith, a Confederate officer, and Frances Lubbock, the Texas Governor. His son, Sam Houston, Jr., was sent home after being wounded in the Battle of Shiloh. Houston's health declined, in April 1863, and he died, on July 26, 1863, at 70 years old.

Personal Life

In January 1829, then Houston was Governor of Tennessee, he married 19 year old Eliza Allen, which only lasted 11 weeks. Eliza refused to sanction divorce. Houston resigned as governor and went to live with the Cherokee family for three years. In 1830, Houston married Tiana Rogers, the daughter of Chief John Rogers, a Scots-Irish trader, and Jennie Due, sister of Chief John Jolly, in a Cherokee ceremony. Tiana was a widower with two children. Houston and Tiana first met when she was 10 years old. The two lived together for many years. Tennessee Society disapproved of the marriage because he was still legally married to Eliza Anna Houston. Tiana declined to go to Texas with Houston. In 1832, Tiana remarried but later died of pneumonia, in 1838.

After becoming President of Texas, in 1837, he then acquired a divorce from Eliza.

Houston married for the third time, on May 9, 1840, to 21 year old Margaret Moffette Lea of Marion, Alabama. They had eight children. The Houston's had several homes; they used the one on Trinity Bay continuously (1840-1863).

In order to qualify for property under Mexican Law, Houston had to be baptized Catholic. By 1854, Margaret had spent 14 years trying to convert Houston to be a Baptist - he finally agreed to convert and agreed to an adult baptism. Houston was baptized on November 19, 1854.

<u>Santa Anna</u>
February 21, 1794 - June 21, 1876

His Most Serene Highness
Antonio Lopez de Santa Anna

Daguerreotype of General Santa Anna, c. 1853

8th President of Mexico

In office: April 20, 1853 - August 5, 1855
Preceded by: Manuel Maria Lombardini
Succeeded by: Martin Carrera

In office: May 20, 1847 - September 15, 1847
Preceded by: Pedro Maria de Anaya
Succeeded by: Manuel de la Peña y Peña

In office: March 21, 1847 - April 2, 1847
Preceded by: Valentin Gomez Farias
Succeeded by: Pedro Maria de Anaya

President of the Mexican Republic

In office: June 4, 1844 - September 12, 1844
Preceded by: Valentin Canalizo
Succeeded by: José Joaquin de Herrera

In office: May 14, 1843 - September 6, 1843
Preceded by: Nicolas Bravo
Succeeded by: Valentin Canalizo
In office: October 10, 1841 - October 26, 1842
Preceded by: Francisco Javier Echeverria
Succeeded by: Nicholas Bravo

In office:: March 20, 1839 - July 10, 1839
Preceded by: Anastasio Bustamante
Succeeded by: Nicolas Bravo

President of the United Mexican States

In office: April 24, 1834 - January 27, 1935
Vice President: Valentin Gomez Farias
Preceded by: Valentin Gomez Farias
Succeeded by: Miguel Barragan

In office: October 27, 1833 - December 15, 1833
Vice President: Valentin Gomez Farias
Preceded by: Valentin Gomez Farias
Succeeded by: Valentin Gomez Farias

In office: June 18, 1833 - July 5, 1833
Vice President: Valentin Gomez Farias
Preceded by: Valentin Gomez Farias
Succeeded by: Valentin Gomez Farias

In office: May 17, 1833 - June 4, 1833
Vice President: Valentin Gomez Farias
Preceded by: Valentin Gomez Farias
Succeeded by: Valentin Gomez Farias

Vice President of the Mexican Republic

In office: April 16, 1837 - March 17, 1839
President: Anastasio Bustamante
Preceded by: Valentin Gomez Farias
Succeeded by: Nicolas Bravo

Personal Details

Born: February 21, 1794
Xalapa, Veracruz, New Spain

Died: June 21, 1876 (aged 82)
Mexico City, Mexico

Resting Place: Panteon del Tepeyac, Mexico City

Political Party: Liberal (until 1833)
Conservative (from 1833)

Spouse(s):
Maria Ines de la Paz Garcia (m. 1825; died 1844)
Maria de los Dolores de Toast (m. 1844)
Awards: Order of Charles III, Order of Guadalupe

Nickname: The Napoleon of the West

Military Service

Allegiance: Kingdom of Spain, Mexican Empire
United Mexican States

Years of Service: 1810 - 1855

Rank: General

Battles/wars:
Mexican War of Independence
Spanish attempts to reconquer Mexico
Casa Mata Plan Revolution
Zacatecas rebellion of 1835
Texas Revolution
Pastry War
Mexican-American War

Chapter Ten
Santa Anna
February 21, 1794 - June 21, 1876

Antonio de Padua Maria Serverino Lopez de Santa Anna Y Perez de Lebron, usually known as Santa Anna... he was a prominent figure in Mexican politics who served as President of Mexico several times. He has been called "The Man of Destiny."

He played a big role in the fall of the first Mexican Empire, the fall of the first Mexican Republic, the promulgation of the Constitution of 1835, the establishment of the Centralist Republic of Mexico, the Texas Revolution, the Pastry War, the promulgation of the Constitution of 1843 and the Mexican American War. He was known for switching sides between the Liberal Party and Conservative Party - coming into power twice in the Liberal Party. He played a part in discarding the Liberal Constitution of 1824, in 1835, and restoring it, in 1847. He was also known for his dictatorial rule by using the military to dissolve Congress multiple times. During his last presidency, he began to go under the title of "His Most Serene Highness." Santa Anna's legacy became viewed as negative, with historians and many Mexicans, as one of those who failed the nation.

His rule lasted from 1832 to 1853 and resulted in the loss of Texas and military failures during the Mexican

American War. He kept prolonging the war and, after the war was over, he continued to alienate national territories to the Americans through the Gadsden Purchase of 1853. Santa Anna was overthrown and exiled, in 1855, through the Liberal Plan of Ayutla. An elderly Santa Anna was allowed to return to the nation by President Sebastian Lerdo de Tajada, in 1874, where he died in relative obscurity, in 1876.

Early Life

Santa Anna was born on February 21, 1794, in Xalapa (New Spain), to a respected Spanish family. They were not a wealthy family but the men held second rank royal and clerical positions. Santa Anna's father was a university graduate and a lawyer. Santa Anna's mother favored his choice of a military career rather than his father's choice of a shopkeeper. His mother's friendly relation with the Intendant (Governor) of Veracruze secured Lopez de Santa Anna's military appointment. Santa Anna had four sisters and two brothers - which his sister, Francisca, and brother, Manuel, also joined the Royal Army.

Career

Lopez de Santa Anna, being a young military officer, during a time of war, was a way that a middle class man could vault from obscurity to a position of leadership. Santa Anna distinguished himself in battle, which led him to a path of national political career. Over his career, he was a strongman wielding both his military and political power like others who emerged in the wake of Spanish American Wars of Independence.

War of Independence
1810-1821

In Santa Anna's early military career, he fought the insurgency for independence and also joined the insurgency against the Spanish crown, showing his many changes of position in his lifetime. In June 1810, at 16 years old, Santa Anna joined the Fijo de Veracruz Infantry Regiment.

The Mexican War lasted until 1821. Lopez de Santa Anna, a Creole military officer, fought for the crown against the mixed-race insurgents for independence. In 1811, Lopez de Santa Anna was wounded in his left hand by an arrow during the campaign while fighting under Colonel Arredondo. In 1813, he served in Texas against the Gutierrez-Magee Expedition and the Battle of Madina; afterwards, he was cited for bravery. He was promoted to Second Lieutenant, in 1812, and then to First Lieutenant at the end of that year. During that time, Lopez de Santa Anna witnessed Arredondo's counterinsurgency policy of mass executions.

Lopez de Santa Anna, along with the Royalist Officer Agustin de Iturbide, changed sides in 1821 and allied with insurgent Vincente Guerrero fighting for independence under the Plan of Iguala. The changed circumstances in Spain, where liberals ousted Ferdinand VII, led to the beginning of implementing the Spanish Liberal Constitution of 1812.

Rebellion Against the Mexican Empire of Iturbide
1822-1823

Iturbide rewarded Lopez de Santa Anna command of the Port of Veracruz then subsequently removed him from his post. Lopez de Santa Anna rose to rebel, in December 1822, against Iturbide. He rebelled because Iturbide had dissolved the Constituent Congress. He promised to support free trade with Span, an important principle for his home region of Veracruz. Iturbide had loyal military who could hold their own against the rebels in Veracruz.

The former insurgent, Vicente Guerrero, and Nicolas Bravo, who had supported Iturbide's Plan de Iguala, returned to their home base in Mexico and rebelled against Iturbide. The commander of the forces in Veracruz, who fought against the rebels, changed sides and joined the rebels. The new coalition proclaimed the "Plan of Casa Mata" that would call for the end of the monarchy, to restore the Constituent Congress and creation of a republic and a federal system.

Lopez de Santa Anna was no longer the main player and sought to regain his position as leader by marching forces from Veracruz to Tampico, then to San Luis Potosi proclaiming his role as the "Protector of the Federation."

Michoacán, Quero Taro and Guanajuato met to decide their own position about the federation. Lopez de Santa Anna pledged his military forces to the protection of the key areas. This is another example, in his career, where he placed himself as head of a movement so it would become an instrument of his advancement.

Lopez de Santa Anna and the Early Mexican Republic

In 1823, Lopez de Santa Anna was sent to command in Yucatan. At that time, the capital of Yucatan's Merida and the port city of Campeche were in conflict. Cuba, a Spanish colony, was the closest trade partner to Yucatan. Lopez de Santa Anna too it upon himself to plan a landing force from Yucatan to Cuba.

He envisioned the colonist would welcome the liberators, especially himself. 1,000 Mexicans were on ships ready to go when word came that the Spanish were reinforcing their colony so, the invasion was called off.

General Guadalupe Victoria, a former insurgent and Liberal Federalist, became the first president of the Mexican Republic, in 1824, following the creation of the Federalist Mexican Constitution of 1824.

There was considerable political conflict during the election of 1828, in which Lopez de Santa Anna became involved with. Even before the election, there was turmoil in Mexico with some affiliated with the "Scottish Rite Masons" plotting a rebellion and "The Liberal York Masons" and the expulsion of the U.S. Minister in Mexico, Joel Roberts Poinsett, a promoter of Federal Republicanism in Mexico. Lopez de Santa Anna threw his support to the Liberals. In Veracruz, the governor threw his support to the Rebels. In the aftermath of the Rebellion's failure, Lopez de Santa Anna, as Vice-Governor, stepped into the governorship.

In 1828, Lopez de Santa Anna and Lorenzo de Zavala supported the Hero of Insurgency, Vicente Guerrero, who was a candidate for the presidency but, Manuel Gomez Pedraza won the indirect elections for the presidency.

Even before all the votes had been counted, in September 1828, Lopez de Santa Anna rebelled against the election results, in support of Guerrero. He called for the nullification of the election results and for a new law expelling Spanish Nationals from Mexico. He believed they were in the league with Mexican Conservatives.

Juan Alvarez joined Lopez de Santa Anna's Rebellion and the governor of the State of Mexico. Lorenzo de Zavala, under a threat of arrest, fled to the mountains and organized his own rebellion against the Federal Government. Zavala brought the fighting right into the Capital.

President Elect Gomez Pedraza resigned and left the country, then Guerrero became the President of Mexico and Lopez de Santa Anna gained prominence as a national leader in his role to oust Gomez Pedraza. Gomez was in favor of Lopez de Santa Anna to invade Cuba. If successful or not, Mexico might ride himself of an undesirable pest, namely Santa Anna.

In 1829, Spain made a final attempt to retake Mexico. Lopez de Santa Anna made his mark in the Early Republic by leading forces that defeated the Spanish Invasion to reconquer Mexico. Spain invaded Tampico with a force of 2,600 soldiers. The defeat of the Spanish Army not only increased Lopez de Santa Anna's popularity but also consolidated the independence of the New Mexican Republic. Lopez de Santa Anna became a hero and, from then on, he styled himself "The Victor of Tampico" and "The Savior of Patria." Then, he would also name himself "The Napoleon of the West."

President Guerrero left the capital to lead a counter rebellion in southern Mexico and Anastasio Bustamante became president. Guerrero was captured and executed after as summery trail, in 1831.

January 1, 1830, was when Bustamante took over the presidency. Bustamante had promised an effective administration and increased import and export taxes but, the revenues were spent on administrative expenses and military. On top of the increased revenues, Bustamante's government borrowed funds from lenders. His government jailed political dissenters.

In 1832, Lopez de Santa Anna declared himself a rebellion against Bustamante and seized the custom's revenue Veracruz. The bloody conflict ended with the resignation of Bustamante's cabinet and an agreement was brokered for new elections, in 1833. Lopez de Santa Anna won handily.

Absentee President
1833-1835

In April 1833, Lopez de Santa Anna was elected president. Although wanting the title, he was not interested in governing. According to Mexican historian Enrique Krauze, governing annoyed him, bored him and maybe even frightened him. Vice President Valentin Gomez Farias took over governing while Santa Anna retired to his hacienda in Veracruz.

The Bustamante government left the nation with an empty Treasury and 11 million pesos in debt. He couldn't cut back on the expenditures on the army and other revenues so, the government targeted the Roman Catholic Church… who supported Bustamante's government so, targeting that institution seemed to be the logical move. A 10% tax on agricultural production was abolished and the church property and finances were seized. The Pontifical University of Mexico was closed and the church's role in education was reduced.

In 1833, Gomez Farias organized the Hijar-Padres Colony to bolster a non-mission civilian settlement. This secondary colony was to help defend Alta California against Russian colonial ambitions from the trading post at Fort Ross. The liberal Catholic Priest, José Maria Luis Mora, who was selling church property, was the key to "transforming" Mexico into a liberal, progressive nation of small land owners. The sale of nonessential church property brought in much needed revenue and the Army was also targeted because it was the largest single expenditure in the national budget. Lopez de Santa Anna suggested to reduce the number of battalions as well as generals and brigadiers.

Ley del Caso was a law that was issued to arrest 51 politicians, including Bustamante, for holding "unpatriotic" beliefs and they were ordered to be expelled from the Republic. It was believed by Gomez Farias that Lopez de Santa Anna was the driving force behind the law. With the resistance of the church and the Army, the Plan of Cuernavaca was issued. The plan was called to repeal the Ley del Caso and discouraged tolerance of the influence of the Masonic Lodges where politics were pursued in secrecy. Likely, this was orchestrated by José Maria Tornel and declared void the laws passed by Congress and the local legislatures in favor of the reforms and requested protection and recognition of President Lopez de Santa Anna as the only authority; it would also declare removal from office the deputies and officials who carried out the enforcement of reform laws and decrees and it would also provide military force to help the president in implementing the plan.

Lopez de Santa Anna was persuaded to return to the presidency and Gomez Farias resigned.

<u>Central Republic</u>
1835

The Liberal Reform of Gomez Farias was radical and Lopez de Santa Anna's actions, in allowing the first reform, might have been a test case for Liberalism. At this point, Lopez de Santa Anna was a Liberal.

By giving Gomez Farias responsibility for the reforms, Lopez de Santa Anna could have plausible deniability. He could be watchful and wait to see the reaction to the comprehensive attack on the privileges of the Army and the Roman Catholic Church, as well as the confiscation of church wealth, enacted by the Radical Liberal Congress.

In May 1834, Lopez de Santa Anna ordered that the Civic Militia be disarmed. He urged congress to abolish Ley del Caso that sent liberal's opponents into exile. On May 25, 1834, the Plan of Cuernavaca was published; it called for repeal of the Liberals Reform. On June 12, Lopez de Santa Anna dissolved Congress and made a decision to adopt a new plan. He formed a new Catholic, Centralist, Conservative government.

In an exchange for preserving the church's and the Army's privileges, the church promised a monthly donation, to the government, of 30,000 to 40,000 pesos. With this, the supporters of Lopez de Santa Anna succeeded where the radicals had failed by forcing the church to assist the republics needs with funds and property.

Again, in 1835, Lopez de Santa Anna returned to his hacienda and left Miguel Barragan as acting President. Lopez de Santa Anna replaced the 1824 Constitution with a new document known as "Siete Leyes" (the Seven Laws). Although Lopez de Santa Anna was blamed for the change to Centralism, he was not actually present during any of the deliberations that led to the abolition of the Federalist Charter or the elaboration of the 1836 Constitution.

Texas Revolution
1835-1836

Lopez de Santa Anna repealed the Mexican Constitution, which ultimately led to starting the Revolutionary War.

The reason Lopez de Santa Anna did this was because he said the settlers were not paying taxes or tariffs, stating they were not recipients of services provided by the Mexican Government.

The Texas Department of the Mexican State of Coahuila Y Tejas rebelled, in late 1835, and declared itself independent, on March 2, 1836. Lopez de Santa Anna, under merciless force, marched north to bring Texas back under Mexican control.

His expedition ended in disaster because he wasn't prepared for all the challenges. He forced wealthy men to provide loans to equip his army and picked up ex-convicts, Indians and derelicts for recruits. His army was fighting cold weather and not the right food. He lacked horses, wagons, mules, cattle and their feed. He lacked medical supplies and chaplains to properly bury the dead. Indians were attacking troops who could not keep up.

Lopez de Santa Anna killed 189 Texans and executed 342 Texan prisoners between the Battle of the Alamo, on March 6, 1836, and the Massacre at Goliad, on March 27, 1836. Lopez de Santa Anna's forces did suffer heavy casualties in the battle.

In 1874, in a letter, he stated he had no choice but to kill everyone at the Alamo.

Lopez de Santa Anna stated William B. Travis was the blame for all the violence at the Alamo. He believed Travis was rude and disrespectful towards him; if that didn't happen, he would have allowed Sam Houston to have a presence there. He claimed it was because of Travis' disrespect that led to the demise of his followers.

The Mexican Army's victory over the Alamo brought more time for Sam Houston to gain weapons and ammunition.

Houston's Texian Army completely routed Lopez de Santa Anna's army at the Battle of San Jacinto. The Texian's shouted "Remember Goliad" and "Remember the Alamo." The day after the battle, a small Texan force, led by James Austin Sylvester, captured Lopez de Santa Anna. They found the General dressed in a private's uniform hiding in the marsh.

Texas President David G. Burnet and Lopez de Santa Anna signed the "Treaty of Velasco," which showed Lopez de Santa Anna as the Chief of the Mexican Nation and acknowledged the full entire and perfect independence of the Republic of Texas. In exchange, the Texas Government would see that Lopez de Santa Anna would have safe transport to Veracruz.

The Mexican Government declared that Lopez de Santa Anna was no longer president and the treaty he signed was null and void. The Mexican Congress rejected the treaty.

Redemption, Dictatorship and Exile

Lopez de Santa Anna met President Andrew Jackson after spending time in the U.S. in exile. In 1837, he was allowed to return to Mexico. He was aboard the USS Pioneer and returned to retire to his hacienda in Veracruz.

While in Veracruz, he wrote about his Texas experience and his surrender.

By the age of 35, he had made a huge reputation with his military career and, by 1835, he felt Texas was the biggest threat to Mexico and acted on those threats.

In 1838, Mexico rejected French demands for financial compensation for losses and France sent forces to Veracruz in the "Pastry War." Mexico gave Santa Anna control of the army and ordered him to defend the nation by any means necessary.

After a failed assault engaging the French at Veracruz, Santa Anna was wounded in the leg and hand. Much of his leg was shattered and had to be amputated.

Santa Anna used his war service to re-enter into Mexican politics. Anatasio Bustamante's presidency got worse and the supporters wanted Santa Anna to control the government. Lopez de Santa Anna became president for the fifth time.

The war with France had weakened Mexico and, also, a rebel army led by José de Urrea and José Antonio Mexia were marching towards the capital against Lopez de Santa Anna.

Lopez de Santa Anna ruled Mexico in more of a dictatorial way than he ever had before. In 1842, he directed the military into Texas and inflicted many casualties with no political gain, but Texas began to be persuaded of benefits of annexation by the United States.

Lopez de Santa Anna began raising taxes, trying to restore the Treasury but grew great resistance. Several Mexican states stopped dealing with the government.

Yucatan and Laredo declared themselves as Independent Republics. Santa Anna stepped down from power and fled, in December of 1844. Fearing for his life, he tried to elude capture but, in January 1845, he was apprehended by Native Americans. He was turned over to authorities and was imprisoned. His life was spared but he was exiled to Cuba.

Mexican-American War
1846-1848

In 1846, while Lopez de Santa Anna was exiled to Cuba, Mexican and American troops moved towards the Rio Grande, into the Nueces Strip. The Mexican Army lost 2 major battles. At that point, the return of Lopez de Santa Anna was palatable to make him president again.

In August 1846, Lopez de Santa Anna returned to Mexico from exile having no intentions of becoming president but would use his military experience in the new conflict.

U.S. President James K. Polk had sent agents to secretly meet with Santa Anna, while in exile, to extract a promise from him to lift the blockade off the

Mexican coast. They allowed him to return to broker the deal. When he returned to Mexico and became head of the army, he reneged on the deal and led the fight against the U.S. invasion.

It had only been a year since he was forced out of the Republic but Lopez de Santa Anna was still popular with the Mexican people. Even though with his double dealing and corruption, they felt he was the most reliable person to help Mexico through threats of their country.

President Polk, having no quick resolution to the conflict in the north, authorized an invasion of Central Mexico to take over the capital and force Mexico to negotiate. Lopez de Santa Anna's army was exhausted, ill clothed, hungry and equipped with inferior weapons.

In the "Battle of Buena Vista," on February 22-23, 1847, with two days of hard fighting, Lopez de Santa Anna withdrew from the field of battle, just as complete victory was at hand.

General Winfield Scott's army landed at Veracruz, Lopez de Santa Anna's home ground. Santa Anna quickly moved to engage to protect the capital. Lopez de Santa Anna set defenses at Cerro Gordo but the U.S. Forces outflanked him and defeated Santa Anna's army.

The Battle of Mexico City and the Battle of Chapultepec were hard fought losses and the U.S. Forces took over the capital. Lopez de Santa Anna fought until the bitter end.

President for the Last Time
1853-1855

After the defeat in the Mexican-American War, in 1848, Lopez de Santa Anna went into exile in

Kingston, Jamaica, then two years later he moved to Turbaco, Columbia.

He was invited back, in April 1853, when the conservatives overthrew a weak liberal government. Lopez de Santa Anna was elected president, on March 17, 1853. He gave himself exalted titles; his situation was quite vulnerable. He declared himself "Dictator of Life" with the title of "Most Serene Highness."

His full title was "Hero of the Nation, General of Division, Grand Master of the National and Distinguished Order of Guadalupe, Grand Cross of the Royal and Distinguished Spanish Order of Carlo III and President of the Mexican Republic."

Personal Life

Lopez de Santa Anna was married twice to wealthy women but did not appear at either wedding ceremony. He empowered his future father-in-law as a proxy at his first wedding and a friend at his second. The two marriages were arranged for convenience was one assessment. It was to bring wealth to Lopez de Santa Anna and his lack of attendance appears to confirm it.

In 1825, he married Ines Garcia, the daughter of wealthy Spanish parents of Veracruz. The couple had four children during their marriage.

Two months after the death of his wife, Ines Garcia in 1844, the then 50 year old Lopez de Santa Anna married 16 year old Maria de los Dolores de Tosta. They rarely lived together; de Tosta lived in Mexico City and Lopez de Santa Anna's political and military activities took him all over the country. They had no children together. Several women claimed to have several of his children and Lopez de Santa Anna acknowledged it in his will and made provisions for them.

Later Years and Death

From 1855 to 1874, Lopez de Santa Anna lived in exile in Cuba. He left because he became unpopular after his defeat, in 1848. He participated in gaming and businesses with hopes of getting rich.

He was a fan of cockfighting and had many roosters that he fought with other roosters from all over the world. In the 1850s, he traveled to New York to try and sell a shipment of chicle (gum) to use for buggy tires but was unsuccessful in convincing wheel manufacturers. Although he introduced chewing gum to the United States, he did not make any money from the product. Thomas Adams, an American aide to Lopez de Santa Anna, bought a ton of the chicle from Santa Anna to try and make a substance like rubber from it but, it was unsuccessful. Instead, he helped find the chewing gum industry with a product that he called Chiclets.

In 1865, Lopez de Santa Anna tried to return to Mexico and offered his services during the French Invasion but was refused by Juarez. Later that year, he took a schooner to Gilbert Thompson's home on Stanton Island, New York. Thompson owned the schooner he took. There, Santa Anna tried to raise money for an army to go back and take over Mexico. In 1874, he took advantage of an amnesty issued by President Sebastian Lerdo de Tejada and went back to Mexico. At that time, he was crippled and almost blind. Lopez de Santa Anna died, in his home, in Mexico

City, on June 21, 1876, at the age of 82. He was buried with full military honors in a glass coffin in Panteon del Tepeyac Cemetery.

Legacy

He was highly controversial. In the 2007 biography by Will Fowler, Santa Anna was depicted as "a liberal, a republican, an army man, a hero, a revolutionary, a regional strongman but, never a politician.

He was always more willing to lead an army than to lead his country.

Mexican-American War

Date: April 25, 1846 - February 2, 2848
(1 year, 9 months, 1 week and 1 day)

Location: Texas, New Mexico, California; Northern, Central, and Eastern Mexico; Mexico City

Result: American victory
• Treaty of Guadalupe Hidalgo
• Mexican recognition of U.S. sovereignty over Texas (among other territories)
• End of the conflict between Mexico and Texas

Territorial changes: Mexican Cession
• Mexico cedes to the U.S. present-day California, Texas, New Mexico, Utah, Nevada, Arizona, and parts of Colorado, Oklahoma, Kansas, Nebraska and Wyoming for $15 million

Commanders and Leaders
United States • California Republic • Mexico

James K. Polk ~ Antonio Lopez de Santa Anna
George M. Dallas ~ Mariano Paredes
George Bancroft ~ Manuel Peña
John E. Wool ~ Mariano Arista
John Y. Mason ~ Pedro de Ampudia
William L. Marcy ~ José Flores
Winfield Scott ~ Mariano Vallejo
Zachary Taylor ~ Nicolas Bravo
Stephen W. Kearny ~ José de Herrera
John D. Sloat ~ Andrés Pico
William J. Worth ~ Manuel Armijo
Robert F. Stockton ~ Martin Perfecto de Cos
Joseph Lane ~ Pedro de Anaya
Franklin Pierce ~ Agustin de Iturbide
David Conner ~ Joaquin Rea
Matthew C. Perry ~ Manuel Muñoz
John C. Frémont ~ Gabriel Valencia
Thomas Childs ~ José de Urrea
Henry Burton ~ Juan Almonte
Edward Baker ~ Manuel Micheltorena
Jefferson Davis ~ John Riley
Robert E. Lee ~ Juan Sequin
Ulysses S. Grant
Henry Clay Jr
William B. Ide

Strength
75,532 - 82,000

Casualties and Losses
1,733 killed - 5,000 killed • 4,152 - 20,000 wounded
11,550 dead from disease • 695 - 10,000 missing

Including civilians killed by violence, military deaths from disease and accidental deaths, the Mexican death toll may have reached 25,000 and the American death toll exceeded 13,283.

Chapter Eleven
Mexican-American War

In 1836, during the "Texas Revolution" and the annexation of Texas, which Mexico still considered territory, Mexico would not recognize the "Treaty of Velasco" which was signed by Antonio Lopez de Santa Anna because he was captured at the Battle of San Jacinto.

The Mexican-American War was an invasion by the United States into Mexico, from 1846 to 1848. James K. Polk was elected as President of the United States, in 1844. He was elected on the platform of expanding the U.S. Territory to Oregon, California and Texas by any means. All this territory was Mexican Territory. The boundary between Texas and Mexico was disputed by Mexico. Polk sent a diplomatic mission to Mexico to buy the disputed territory along with California and everything between for $25 million but, the Mexican Government refused to accept. President Polk then sent 80 soldiers across the territory to the Rio Grande, ignoring Mexican demands to withdraw. Mexico interpreted this as an attack and drove the U.S. Forces back on April 25, 1846. Polk used this move to convince Congress to declare war.

The U.S. Forces quickly occupied the capital of Santa Fe de Nuevo, Mexico. They also moved against the Province of Alta, California and then went south.

The U.S. Navy blocked the Pacific Coast in lower Baja, California. Major General Winfield Scott invaded Mexico and captured the capital, Mexico City, in September 1847.

Even though Mexico was defeated on the battlefield, they refused to recognize the loss of territory. Nicolas Trist was the post negotiator and was relieved by President Polk. Trist ignored the order and concluded The 1848 Treaty of Guadalupe Hidalgo. This ended the war and was recognized by Mexico. The U.S. paid $15 million for physical damage of the war and assumed $3.25 million in debt owed by Mexico to the U.S. citizens. Mexico gave up Texas, California, Nevada and Utah. They also gave up parts of Arizona, Colorado, New Mexico and Wyoming. Mexico also accepted the Rio Grande as its border.

President Polk envisioned that this would inspire patriotism among the United States but it brought criticism for the casualties, cost and handedness.

Some scholars see the Mexican-American War as leading to the American Civil War by the debate about extension of slavery into the conquered Mexican area leading to heightened sectional tension.

In Mexico, the war led to political turmoil. Mexico suffered great losses of both civilian and military population. The nation's financial foundation was ruined and half the territory was lost. A group of Mexican writers called it a "state of degradation and ruin."

Credits for Reference

http://en.wikipedia.org/

- wiki/battle_of_the_alamo
- wiki/davy_crockett
- wiki/list_of_alamo_defenders
- wiki/james_bowie
- wiki/william_b_travis
- wiki/antonio_lopez_santa_anna
- wiki/sam_houston
- wiki/battle_of_the_alamo
- wiki/alamo-mission
- wiki/seige_of_the_alamo
- wiki/republic_of_texas
- wiki/mexican_american_war
- p.77 image Gigette, Wikpedia

brittanica.com
- biography/james-bowie
- topic/texas-revolution/santa-anna-responds-alamo
- event/battle-of-the-alamo

https://www.history.com/topics/19thcentury
- davy-crockett
- this-day-in-history/alamo-defender-call-for-help
- new/the-first-shots-of-the-texas-revolution
- this-day-in-history/alamo-texas-battle-ends

About the Author

James R. Bower, retired designer of architectural and mechanical engineering. A U.S. paratrooper, veteran of the '60s and '70s. The president of the Deer Park Art League in Deer Park, Texas.

www.ingramcontent.com/pod-product-compliance
Lightning Source LLC
LaVergne TN
LVHW041853070526
838199LV00045BB/1578